p. 28 → Lorna.
35 → E+E; and 40-41
42 love

*Wrapped Within Again*

# Wrapped Within Again

*New and Selected Poems*

Robert Hilles

Black Moss
2003

© 2003, Robert Hilles

National Library of Canada Cataloguing in Publication

Hilles, Robert, 1951-
    Wrapped within again : new and selected poems / by Robert Hilles.

ISBN 0-88753-384-1

    I. Title.

PS8565.I48W73 2003         C811'.54         C2003-902753-8
PR9199.3.H483W73 2003

Design: Karen Veryle Monck

Published by Black Moss Press at 2450 Byng Road, Windsor, Ontario N8W 3E8. Black Moss books are distributed in Canada and the U.S. by Firefly Books, 3680 Victoria Park Ave., Willowdale, Ont. Canada. All orders should be directed there.

Black Moss would like to acknowledge the generous support of the Canada Council and the Ontario Arts Council for its publishing program.

ONTARIO ARTS COUNCIL
CONSEIL DES ARTS DE L'ONTARIO

Le Conseil des Arts | The Canada Council
du Canada | for the Arts

## *Acknowledgements:*

I am indebted first to the numerous literary magazines that published most of these poems, and second to the publishers that showed faith in my work over the years. Most of these presses are still alive and thriving across the country. They are: Turnstone Press, Sidereal Press, Oolichan Books, Thistledown Press, Wolsak and Wynn, Black Moss Press and River Books. These publishers were also kind of enough to allow me the permission to use these poems even though many of my books remain in print. A version of the poem Generous Waters, previously appeared in *Arc*.

I also thank the various writers and editors who gave me suggestions or support over the years including, Claire Harris, Ron Smith, Patrick O'Rourke, Steven Michael Berzensky, John B. Lee, Don Coles, Christopher Wiseman, Maria Jacobs, Heather Cadsby, Betsy Struthers, Robert Kroetsch, Candace Dorsey, Fred Stenson, Pamela Banting, Roberta Rees, Richard Stevenson, Ted Blodgett, Patrick Lane, Brian Brett, Edna Alford, Joan Clark, Dale Fehr, Bruce Hunter, Catherine Hunter, Anne Szumigalski, Liliane Welch, Weyman Chan, Gay Allison, Geoff Hancock, Jay Ruzesky, Susan Musgrave, Lorna Crozier, Barb Scott, Erin Moure, Gary Geddes, Rhea Tregebov, Mary di Michele, Roo Borson, Kim Maltman, Antonio D'Alphonso, M. Travis Lane, Richard Harrison, Rajinderpal S. Pal, Allan Brown, Jan Zwicky, Charles Noble, Don McKay, Robert Priest, Ken Stange, Roger Greenwald, Paul Wilson, Mona Fertig, Peter Levitt, Shirley Graham, Allan Safarik, Dolores Reimer, George Melnyk, Monty Reid, Robert Billings, Ken Rivard, and any I have forgot.

I also wish to thank my friend and publisher Marty Gervais who has believed in my work over the years. Also a thanks to

David Albahari and Barry Dempster for their support and the suggestions for this selection. I would also like to thank David Albahari for his translation of a number of these poems into Serbian. To the memory of Cathy McKay and for hers and Greg Gerrard's generous support.

Most of all I want to thank my partner and best friend Pearl Luke who besides her many generous editing suggestions, helped with the final selection of the poems included here, and each day helps me believe.

## Table of Contents

*From Look The Lovely Animal Speaks, Turnstone Books, 1980*
    This Poem Leaves No Survivors     13
    The Strength In The Earth Has Left Us     14
    For Isaac Babel     15
    Then     17

*From An Angel In The Works, Oolichan Books, 1983*
    These Old Hands I Speak With     21
    Hands     22
    Deep Structure     23
    This Train Makes No Stops     24
    An Angel In The Works     25
    All My Fathers Have Fantastic Women     26
    Upon Waking I Will Write This Down     28
    Small Fruit     29
    When You Die     30

*From Outlasting The Landscape, Thistledown Press, 1989*
    Heavy     35
    Relation     37
    Words Contain Sleep     39
    Foothills In Winter     40
    Outlasting The Landscape     42
    Tones And Light     44
    After You Sleep I Sleep     45
    Poem Found While Ironing     46
    Something Dangerous     47
    Rush Hour     48
    Stumblings     49
    Matter Is A Sound That Echoes     51
    A Tender Man     53
    This Poem Will Not Harm You     54

*From Finding the Lights On, Wolsak and Wynn, 1991*
    Letters To My Mother: Letter VIII      59
        Letter XII      60
    So Distant, So Near      62
    To You      63
    A Gust Inside A God      64
    Playing Music      65
    Boy In A Choir      66
    God's Moustache      67

*From A Breath At A Time, Oolichan Books, 1992*
    The Numbers Begin      71
    A Breath At A Time      72
    So Holy Is The Mystery      73
    Nothing Is More Temporary      74
    Dead Eyes      75
    God      76

*From Cantos From A Small Room, Wolsak and Wynn, 1993*
    Canto 2: A Sign a Petal Makes      79
    Canto 7: There Are No Accidents Between Lovers      81
    Canto 9: The Dream Canto      84
    Map Of Light      87
    Meandering      89
    God Is The Smallest Object      91

*From Nothing Vanishes, Wolsak and Wynn, 1996*
    Nothing Vanishes      95
    Speaking In Tongues      99
    Chances      101
    Waiting In The Dark      102
    Apples      104
    Tomatoes      105
    Last Words To A Father      107

*From Breathing Distance, Black Moss Press, 1997*
    Ode To Isaac Babel and My Dead Father      111
    Ode To Sakutaro Hagiwara      113

| | |
|---|---|
| Ode To Tadeusz Rosewicz | 115 |
| Ode To Death | 117 |

*From Somewhere Between Obstacles And Pleasure,*
*Black Moss Press, 1999*

| | |
|---|---|
| Shaped By The Wind | 123 |
| The Barking Dogs Of San Miguel II | 124 |
| What Bodies Hold | 127 |
| The Soul's Journey | 128 |
| Heat Locked | 131 |
| In And Out Of Light | 134 |
| Living | 137 |
| A Place To Keep My Words | 139 |
| Two Digits | 141 |
| A Heaven Filled With Snow | 142 |
| Hydrangeas | 143 |

*From Higher Ground, River Books, 2001*

| | |
|---|---|
| Beloved | 147 |
| Higher Ground | 149 |
| The Scientific Measurement Of Love | 151 |
| All In The Family | 154 |
| Singing In Traffic | 155 |
| First Day Of School | 158 |
| Grace Period | 160 |
| Winter | 162 |

*Time Beyond History, New Poems*

| | |
|---|---|
| Time Beyond History | 165 |
| Generous Waters | 167 |
| Austin Contemplates Death | 168 |
| My Father's Bed | 169 |
| For The Record | 170 |
| Chopin's Music | 171 |
| A Peculiar Stretching Of Time | 172 |
| All The White Rooms | 174 |
| Molasses | 175 |

*For Pearl who makes things happen,*
*and*
*for Austin, Breanne, Amanda and Woody,*
*and again*
*for the people in the poems.*

*Look the Lovely Animal Speaks*

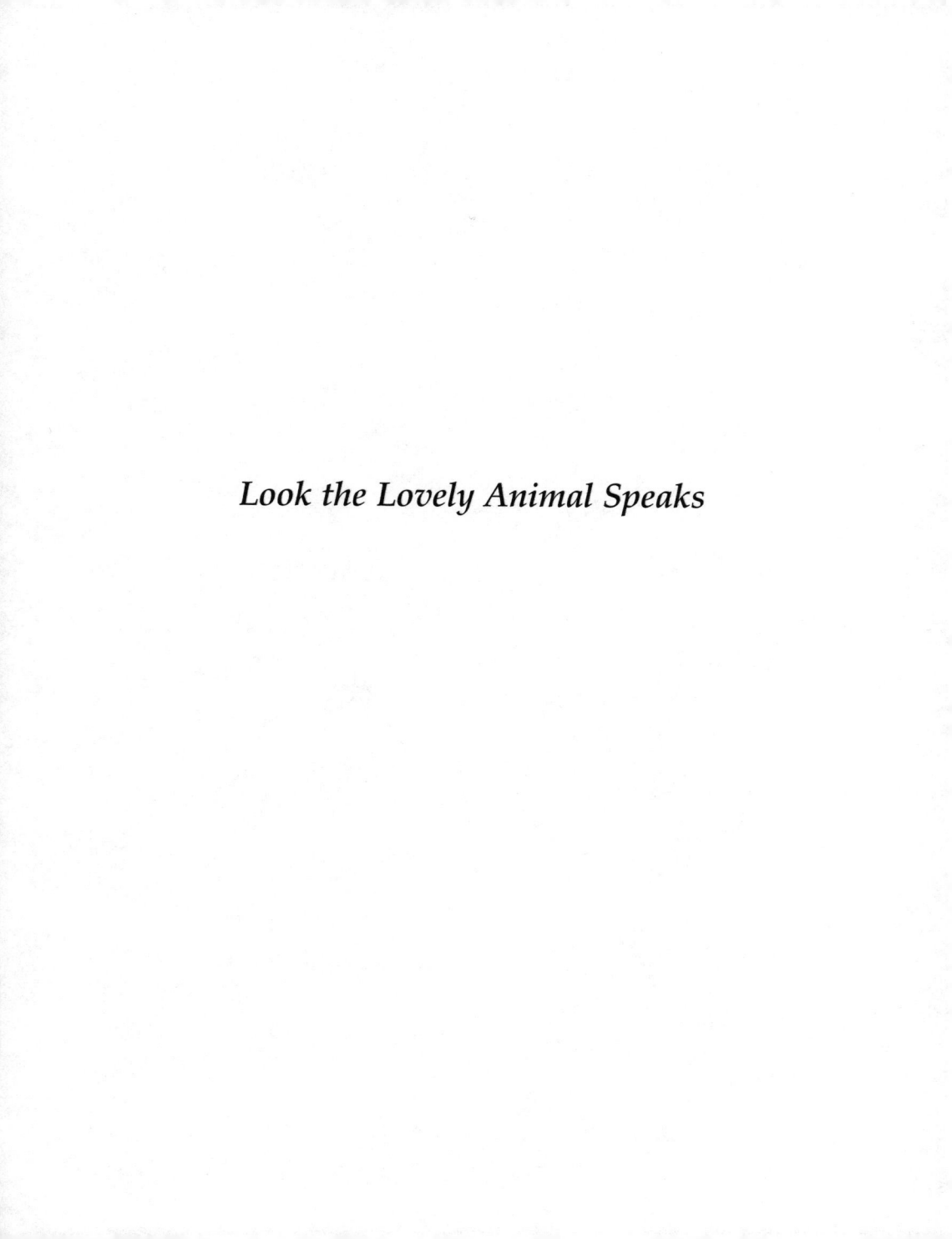

## *This Poem Leaves No Survivors*

this poem collects
things but it
leaves no survivors.
it's not surprising that
you come here
expecting the worst
since we all
carry murder around
like baby pictures in a wallet.
it's too late to scream
this poem is soundproof
and if you try
to tear your
eyes away the page
will wrench them
back.
I didn't want to
resort to this but
you stood too long
jingling your change.

## *The Strength In The Earth Has Left Us*

the strength in the earth
has left us.
my father had a farm
but lost it.
it's now a rifle
range for trigger
happy city kids.
the only thing they'll
ever shoot are plastic skeets.
my father much older
and humbler now
works for the government
keeping their highways clean.
he doesn't know much
about the government or how it
works neither does he care.
all he understands
is that they took his land
and now they pay him
to garden their cement fields.
he feels cheated inside
and the mystery has
long since left his eyes.
he now sits at home
and drinks beer, sleeps
it off and goes to work.
and I his eldest son
will never have a
chance to walk on my own land and
escape the greedy
hands of landlords.

no, I sit in a cheap apartment in Calgary
and lament about how
the strength in the earth
has left us.

## *For Isaac Babel*

a woman sings
a child weeps on a bed
under a stinking heap
of rags.
the streets outside
are muddy like
the souls of the people.

a Cossack walks by.
war knows
no sanctuaries.

there is always time to
dance and sing and stoke the fire.
the smoke is never
remembered it just
drifts toward the sky
like a long border
and the curfews of the eye
are shaped by the
landscapes of sunset and dawn.

## *Then*

poverty teaches no one
it's just dark and small
like a revolver.
always ready to be
the final judge.

I remember dirty walls,
macaroni, television, and
dumping the slop pail.
there was no beauty
you just survived
between paydays.

my father
drank every Friday
and Saturday nights
he lived between
the borders of the day shift
and the night shift.
that was the only
structure I knew.

I know now
that he sold
what little of himself
he had so that I could eat.
what kind of change is that?
where one generation sacrifices
itself so that the next one
can walk on its bones
with a new pair of shoes.

*An Angel in the Works*

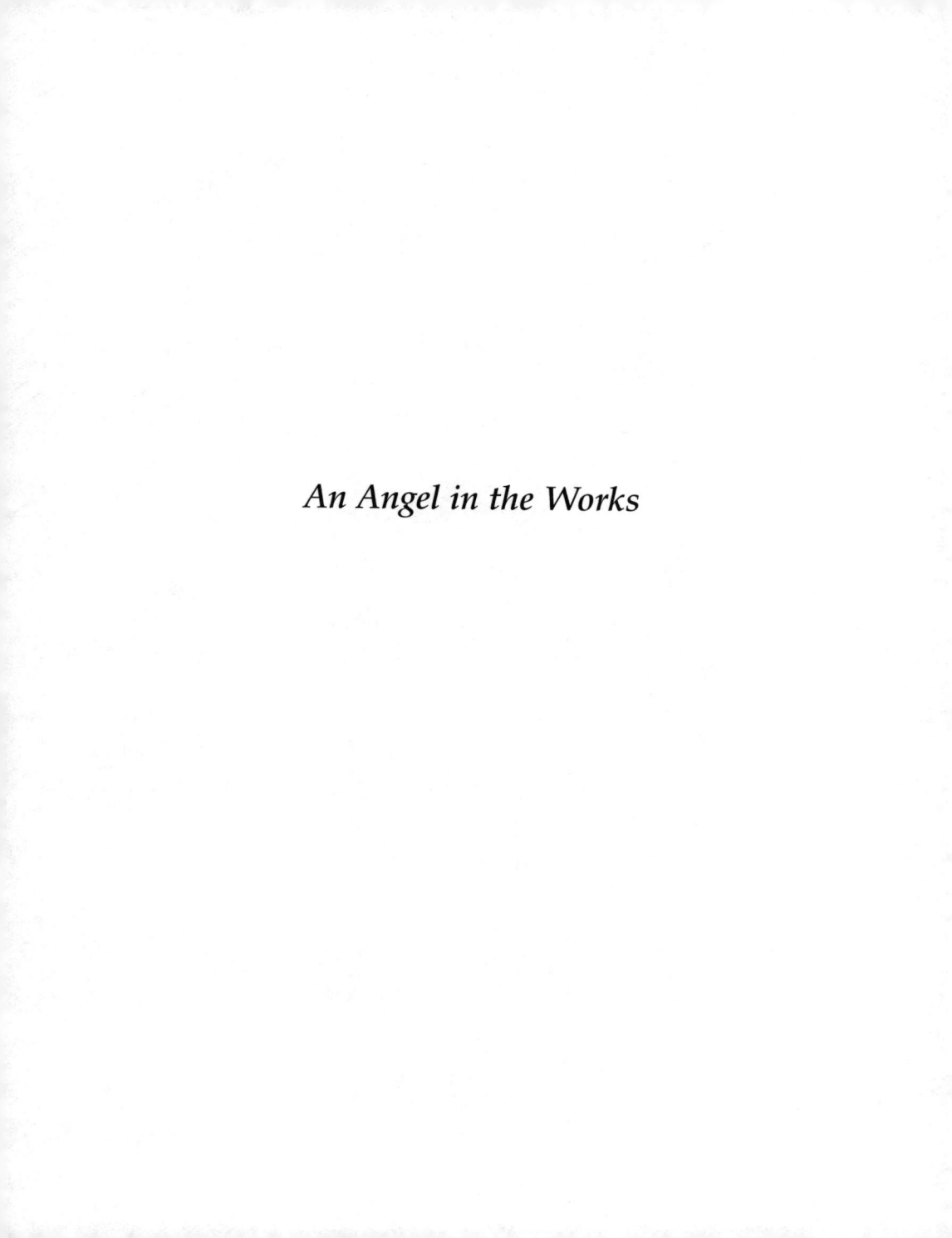

## *These Old Hands I Speak With*

even the most beautiful song
cannot save the voice
we are caught inside
the very sound we breathe
the throat is a graceful prison

our mouths are soft and moist
when they meet and for a moment
we are free from our old awkwardness
and forget all that is impossible
between us

these old hands
have their own intelligence as
they slide across your body
I could never make words do that

## *Hands*

we spend all our lives
warming hands blowing
onto them slapping them
on our legs
only those who wake
out of dark dreams
reach for their hands first
and then for the light
in such a darkness
there is no history beyond faith

in another country
someone has just said goodbye
to a lover of 15 years
their hands together hold a gospel
you sense that they have
spoken something wild and forbidden
and yet those humble hands
tangled together must never
again be tied behind the back
it's like that too in the morning
I wait for your hand on my penis
those soft strokes make me
want to sing in your ear
and to rest my tongue there
between the notes

## *Deep Structure*

there is an echo in every silence

the deep structure is more
than geological memory
more than remembering the form of air
that your lungs translate
or how your fingers assemble knowledge

how many parts do you have to name
before you discover
that you actually bleed
or feel how your emotions dance free
on the tightrope of your backbone

the blood is always contained
it connects joy with pain
everything separates into itself
but still corresponds to
that larger movement
across the expanding landscape

## *This Train Makes No Stops*

for us time can get no shorter

all things begin in violence

and the distance that surrounds us
is imagined and real at the same time
you are hanging up the phone
I am passing a hand through my hair
outside a car horn sounds

things move always outwards and inwards
all motion is the exploration of distance
and a hand carving love is as strong
as a hand carving silence

all of us are nomads as if we were
born on highways
our true longing is for the range
and the hills beyond
where only by moving ever onward
does the world become a place
where we can live

## *An Angel In The Works*
### *for Jack Spicer*

this poem is for you Jack
for you where the sea crashes without ears
where the sky moves without eyes
in a small room I learn new words
and new ways of speaking

we will collapse without songs
the poem must survive
I know that you were not a big man
you wanted the poem to come on its own
I want to tell you a story
about two lovers alone in a room
each is dancing in their own footsteps
they continue to dance
even now as I look in

there is no music
nor need there be
there is an angel in the works
and the lovers are dancing

## *All My Fathers Have Fantastic Women*

at daybreak the sun is alone
trying to bury the horizon
there is no voice
no song, no landscape
this is the way
all my fathers have planned it
they become the day
singing in voices primitive and electronic
there has been a death in the family

I slip back behind the house
frightened of the growing light
I feel my throat harden
my hands crumble
there is dried mud on my feet
I can see all my fathers
they have fantastic women
they are standing in a circle
one of them speaks:

>   When we leave,
>   this ground will poison its children
>   the grass will shrivel
>   the trees will die
>   the air will disappear.

I have no way of dying
I have seen all my fathers
and they have fantastic women
they drift past me like a memory
we have lived together in this small madness
they are prepared to teach me nothing
they are speculating on their own death
all my fathers have fantastic women
that is the magic

## *Upon Waking I Will Write This Down*

it's not how small things are
or who the lovers are
the pain is always inside
the particles become smaller and smaller
and yet there is no entrance
no way to get inside

the world is made of mundane things
objects moved around rooms
furniture piled against a wall
the colours trapped in their own name
you can say it, shape it
with your lips but can
never own it

things are shapeless
they fall apart in your hand
you cannot know what
they are or how they feel
even your own body
floats inside rooms
barely touching the floor
you think you control
the steps but find yourself
at strange destinations
your stomach empty and
your legs mysteriously tired

everything is contrived but real
what I give you is imagined
but pretends to truth
what I say is real
but was learned in dreams

## *Small Fruit*

we soon forget the rage
that is never still
even as the vegetation dies
around us and the rivers
turn more and more black
you must suckle small fruit
and charm its sweet nectar
on your tongue
you must eat slowly
let the teeth burn as they chew
the hunger is still there
over and over
only you can feel it inside
the hollow throat

## *When You Die*

across the road
there is a garden
and when you die
the dust you inhabit
will be spread over that ground
so thinly it will never
again hold an image

When you are home at night
with the windows closed
and the heat turned down
do you bring small flowers to your lips
while the light crawls into the room
as if from a darker world

the soft blood
rests in old veins
I reach around you
to protect an impression
I once had
I tell you of my father
how he still holds me
in his hands
and how he washes flowers until
they shed their pale colours

we stand together
and reach for our separate clothes
as we long for rain
to make the escape more real
we long to hold something
important in our hands
and for each heart to be
capable of more than just beating
alone in its prison of ribs

*Outlasting the Landscape*

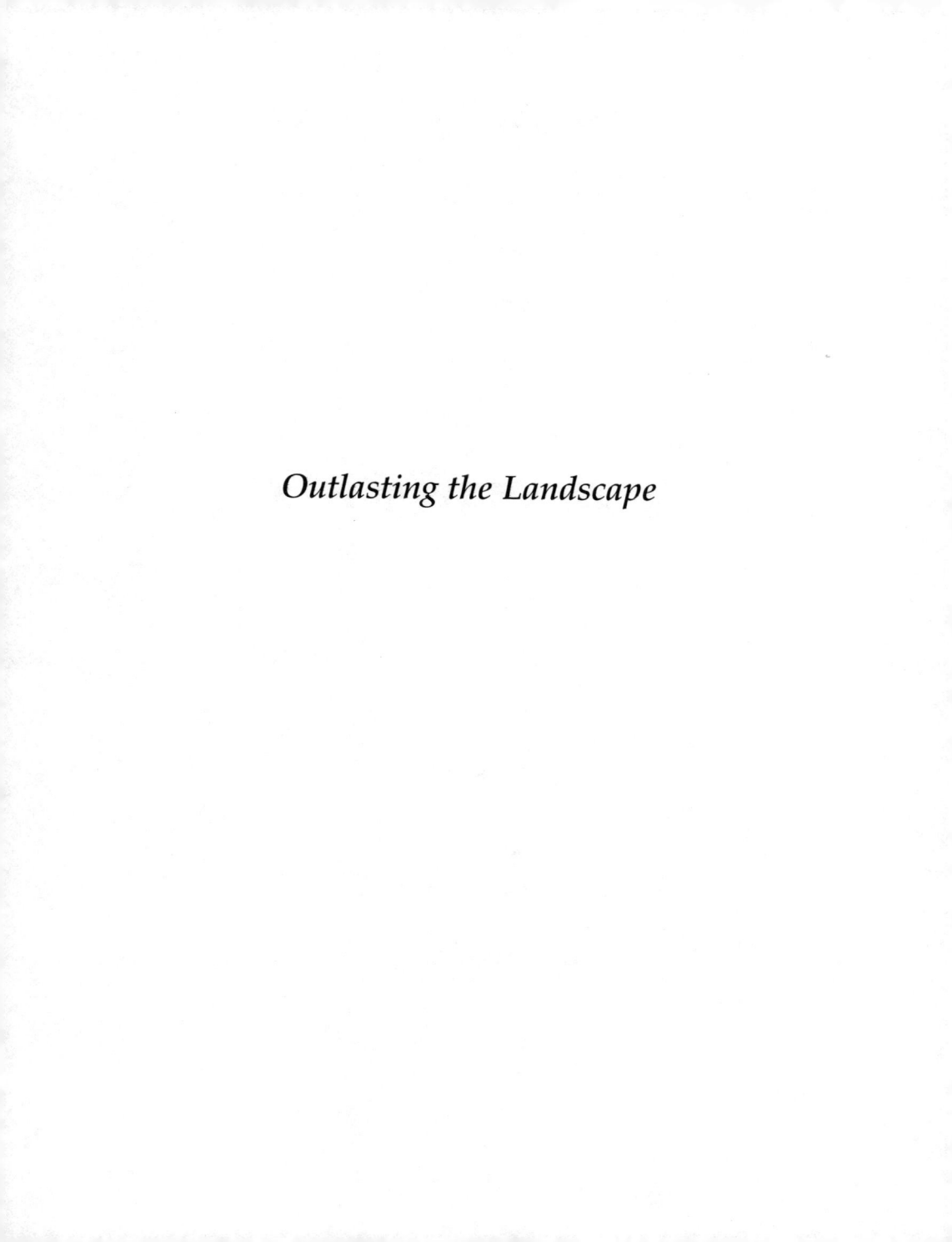

## *Heavy*

A father listens to
his daughter cry herself to sleep and
knows the weight of the future,
how children elsewhere
huddle in fear of the world
their faces unwashed, untouched—centuries
of despair filling their love.

He fumbles with disk operating
systems, the plain magic of green
letters blinking on a tiny screen
creating new reflexes to be practiced
and mastered. Children survive us living in a
parenthetical reality
where love is discovered only in folklore.

None of the past explains the love
he has for his daughter or this moment
when she is the most vulnerable.
He can see it in her eyes
the way she feels everything,
her dreaming still outside
the framework of guilt. He watches
her pull herself up and stand
proudly as if all of her life
meant only that one act.
A filling of herself with pride and success.
There are no small miracles for her.
Each day is a different discovery
the world moved one step closer to her.
She is big in it.
The light making everything possible.
She can't turn back.

He has come to shape a different love
for her. One he can't get out of.
There is no divorce possible. They
are sometimes as great as each other.
Telling their short history with their eyes.
They have grown toward peace, a longing
inside that seems so precise, as if
every nerve knew it. The father reads
stories to his daughter, each one
ends completely and abruptly as if
there were no words left to fit in.
He knows the world is otherwise
fractional and chaotic.
He wants her to see that the stories
are not stories at all but an expression
of love passed between
parent and child, a longing to stretch out
and offer some magnificent account
of how her life came to be.

Today he feeds her eggs
and she frowns. In thirty years
there will be time to discover
the meaning of all this. Now it seems
so practical to call what doesn't fit
love and to accept each other
as an alibi for something else.

## *Relation*

I have expected dancers to emerge
from the words themselves.
To find in your praise the clear taste
of an unexpected kiss.
I know how to tear down this house
board by board
how each corner is formed out of the strength
of its opposite corner.
How the wood forms more than rooms.
The roof bends but does not give in to the elements.
If I tear down this place,
I will lose the power that holds it together.

We wait for our lives to bloom like flowers
that have some notion of their own biology.
Our daughter seems to know us better than
ourselves. Our voices are different and
yet she is learning to speak as I speak.
The delight mutual.
*Oh, where is the air we lie beneath?*
*Where is the water that builds*
*a canopy above us? Our shouting words*
*filling an open solitude.*

This morning you left early
the bed larger in your absence.
I lie awake waiting for Breanne to cry,
crying is what lets us love.
I hear crying from every corner of the house
and beyond more and more tears as if
everything in the universe were crying.

Tear after tear changing the scale
of the universe until some insignificant event like
the furnace cutting in squelches it.

We are changed by our need to stay the same
listening at the door of some warm place
knowing that heaven is as small as hands.

## *Words Contain Sleep*

Our words contain more than sleep. They pass between things. Language seeing itself reborn. The windows contain the light. It does not pass through but lives in the glass, shining out in both directions. Sleep has a structure outside of words. And we are too close to our own sleep, waking at night hallucinating. Sleep pulls us out. It is a costume we dress our terror in. It is the unseen existing in light. Nothing remains when we wake but a few random names or images. Sleep has no fragrance. When we dream, our bodies are suddenly immune to meaning. We remember only certain things upon waking. Our bodies petrified by the reality there.

## *Foothills In Winter*

I hoist Breanne onto the sleigh and watch a lone skier in the distance. Stride after stride. I imitate myself and Breanne smiles as the sun turns us invisible in the snow. There is no sound of traffic to change the notes of the world even though the city waits a mile away. We are cut off and there are few lines to separate us from each other's heart. I pull her up and down small hills through a thin stand of poplars; below us I can count the streets to our house; the rooms opening to our absence. I lift Breanne to show her the city but she turns to my face; her sight still concerned with things up close.

This place we retreat to is between city and mountains. A no man's land of grass, snow, and a few ghostly trees. It makes me feel perfect inside. Our time together is too short. In the spring, the snow will disappear but this place will be the same. We will hunt through the crocuses; they will replace the words we cannot exchange. Breanne finds my moustache and begins to pull. Our positions never stay the same; sometimes I cannot place her face or her eyes; they seem too different, too much my own obsession. Sometimes I watch her chase the cat and I imagine our descendants caught in the lightning of the same madness.

I pull Breanne away from the city, snow intoxicating in its midday glare. The mountains larger and nearer in winter are caught quietly in bending sunlight. We disappear beneath the snow, memory too physical to follow us. Birds in their winter costumes seem to fly without their wings, their eyes X-raying the snow for food, spring. They surround us, and Breanne laughs, her stresses new, her syllables beyond anything I could teach her. She watches me dance into a cloud, watches the snow cling to my clothes as I pull her toward the mountains and spring.

I fall down and again Breanne laughs and the snow floats around her, melting against her warm skin. A squirrel (a refugee from summer) chatters on a nearby poplar branch, and we play, our bodies like precious instruments, our lungs filled with the notes of this moment. We begin singing without knowing the song. The trees leading us into the chorus. We play out the world, make the sky refuse us. Tenderness opens inside like the first crocuses of the new year. Breanne has brought me to this place, and has taught me how to look beyond the city, beyond the mountains, into her face.

## *Outlasting The Landscape*

This afternoon the sun burns through
the trees in the backyard, and I wait
for you to return home.
I look at your picture across
the room and cannot imagine
how I confuse anger with love.
Things in the room get blamed.
The table not neat enough:
windows dark too soon.

Breanne's toys crowd us out
of the living room, spread
to our bedroom where we flee locking the door.
Both of us too tired and sore to embrace,
the light wrong, the phone's shrill.

Our daughter's name is the only
protection we can provide her.
This world more fragile than
the few words that describe it.
When we argue as if we really understood
each other's intent that is when we are
in danger of outlasting the landscape,
making the world less noble or exact.
Along one wall, we could hang our future,
show Breanne how the world
will look when she is older.

When I am angry,
the door opens to the left,
pictures tilt the afternoon light.
Soon the door will open and you will enter,
Breanne in your arms. I will be
washing dishes and as you stand holding
her I will know what anger destroys.
I will take your coat and lay it across
a chair, small offering in a larger life.
Your shoes solid as they fall.

## *Tones And Light*

It is not a sacrifice to love you, my daughter, a miracle I cannot describe. There is no sunset I can replay to you in words. Your thoughts still dominated by the perils of walking. Some mornings you sing to me and I am moved by how your songs echo my silence. Inside I try to be harder, to make it in a world where tenderness is a weakness. Your eyes bury my doubt. And I can't stop thinking about the newborn saved by a German shepherd curling around the baby to keep her warm. How animals transcend us. Our intentions too calculated and good.

I save advice for you that I have practiced on lovers, friends. But I know that for you it will be all wrong. A father tries too hard. Of course, your dreams will be different than I imagine. The music there as foreign as my presence. I can offer no protection. Not even advice on how to avoid the fears. My past is too much for me to empty. I cannot fill your life. I am distant. Calling from another time. My daughter is not you. This is not our lives I describe but a fantasy I cannot forget.

I struggle to name what I cannot see.

## *After You Sleep I Sleep*

When I went to wake you, I found you sitting in your crib. I was surprised to find you already awake, so quiet, as though you knew I was still sleeping. And I saw you differently. Not as my small daughter, too fragile yet for this complicated world. But as one who knows how your father sleeps without any trees in his dreams. How some days he is too tired to hear you cough at night. His pillow hiding his face like a mask. This morning I could not speak to you my head still filled with your solitude. Someday you will kiss me a certain way, and I will know that my years are more a hindrance than an aid. I will know that you see all the trees I cannot dream. Forgive my hands as they lifted you this morning from your peace. I cannot explain yet why I did that. Or why this poem will not let me speak of it now. Content to confuse as only words and poems can.

## *Poem Found While Ironing*

A freight train frightens my daughter.
The weight of the imagination thins at
this altitude. The sky refuses to
disappear. Breanne climbs ahead and
behind me, her shoes intersecting with
the earth at strange angles. She knows
how to vanish. How the spring air fills
with the echoes of birds and water. At
the first crocus on the trail,
she grows ten years. With her hands,
she forms the shape of apples.
I carry her back to the car.
Her years disappearing as we
approach the parking lot.
Our hands need cleaning,
need to make sense out of power.

## *Something Dangerous*

The man in the next cell is your father. In his sleep he calls you names. The warden sends you notes which describe how your father looked on the day you were born. Describe the colour of shirts he liked to wear. The kinds of places he used to stop for a drink. The warden spells your name wrong. He wants you to confess to having prior knowledge of your birth. You love him and want to tear the flesh off his skeleton. To watch his body melt into a cry of love. You have studied the patience of others, learned from your father the reasons for your imprisonment. His voice is the flutter of a moth's wings around your cell's light. So fragile is the meaning of anything dangerous.

## Rush Hour

The days working
outnumber the days at rest.
Sleep a sudden memory in the
morning when traffic is too
slow, when images of urban
sprawl are too horrible to forget.
The nights outlast
our sleep, our dreams disturbed
by a teething child.

On the way to work,
you watch a child
cross the street and
paradise seems impossible.
Our commitments too casual
to lead us there.

At work, you drink coffee and
watch the madness of traffic
from forty floors up.
The body paradoxical
manufacturing its own terror
and delight.

This universe we protest
dumbfounds us. Our patience
with god grows shorter.
We have lost
our reflexes, our instincts
transformed into user-friendly
software.
Our voices more
mechanical each day.

## *Stumblings*

He stumbles in after a day of drinking
and I am angry from worrying that he
was lost in Calgary, a strange city for him, or
worse that he was beaten up and robbed in one
of the seedy bars he seeks out.
My father drinks until the pain disappears.
He tells himself the same
stories until he passes out. His strength
is held inside as in a small clay pot.

This winter when he came to visit
I noticed for the first time how
he walks bent over. His tired eyes caved-in
against the light. Every morning he
shoveled the walk or talked to our neighbours
about the bush. I know he can't leave there
and sometimes I am a stranger—out of focus.
In the city, there is too much cement
and all the trout are gone from the Bow River.

He doesn't hear the screams beyond
the walls of the guest bedroom. Instead, love exists
in some other twisted and exaggerated way.
He holds my hand after a day of too much drinking,
and I cannot explain to him the worthiness of his life.

We try to protect one another,
to understand how each violin string
rejects the darkness, to find again
the lights of the world held in a steady state.

I dream of physicists who try to tell
the particles apart. The world frozen in
a tragic order. The chaos more human
than anything. The behavior of children and
parents equaled by the tragedy of love.

I can only think about one thing at a time.
My mind tired from the fighting, from too many nights
trying to avoid the glare of the TV and his
still eyes. The terror always there. Modern
folktales surrounding us and holding us apart.
I cannot make myself love his contradictions,
yet I am nothing but words that have good intentions,
safe, clean, and acceptable.
I want praise and a place to sleep where
the anger does not last all night. I can hear
him walking around in the dark, bumping into
my old typewriter, left too close
to the top of the stairs.
In another time I would have been frightened
by his stumblings. Now I can only guess
why he suffers himself so much.

Our lives more than boundaries apart.
Sometimes we are father and son. Other times,
our purposes are a paradox of wonder and disbelief.
These are hard times between
the beginning and ending of a world.

## *Matter Is A Sound That Echoes*

In a Toronto hotel,
I watch a TV evangelist,
and I am reminded that my mother
still believes in evangelists.
Their words releasing her from torment.
He is describing how
comfortable heaven will be and I
imagine rows of expensive condominiums
perfectly manicured. I imagine
limousines with the unrepentant forced
to drive. The golf course is only
three blocks away and I have
a three stroke handicap. Everyone of course
dresses in white. But heaven does not
belong to bodies or matter. It is
anti-matter. A weapon that space uses.

Matter is a sound that echoes and my mother's
fears are now mine. Some days
any god will do as long as he is
righteous. Other days the world seems
heavy enough without external forces.
Now the evangelist is giving instructions on
how to make it into the kingdom of god.
I remember my mother weeping with
self-doubt, worried that she might be
unworthy of his kingdom. I could see
then that doubt was a delicate thing
and hinged on the power of words. Or I
should say, I can see that now

hearing this minister
use words as though they were a
hypnotist's watch. The twentieth
century is about to fade into oblivion
and my childhood with it. We have
become the sounds we hear at night on TV.
Countries identified by an insane pride.

The evangelist is pleading with me
to send money. He knows I can
save my mother by phoning the supreme
being and offering my body for
scientific research. Yet I cannot
turn off the TV. As though somewhere
in all the garbled nonsense I might
be able to retrace myself out of this
century either backwards or forwards
and find my mother, whole, singing in
the bush of Northwestern Ontario,
singing as if everyone's life depended
upon it.

Oh mother, everyone was wrong.
The world doesn't add up without your
beliefs. Your god is easy to mock and
that bothers me. Somewhere I have
missed the whole point.
My thoughts echo back toward the
traffic on Yonge Street.
The sound of a dying world.

## *A Tender Man*

A tender man who understands machinery.
He speaks with his hands lifting
a cigarette from a black dish. Words
are a necessary evil one needs to earn a
living. At night he watches TV with the
sound turned down. Lives and passions,
flickering in the darkness, messages
that need no translation.
His legs bend stiffly as he climbs the
stairs at my house. He hates stairs.
He drinks too much as though his
gentleness has cost him everything.

My father was not a waiter in any fancy
restaurant, his addition is bad,
his life a necessary maze of wrong turns.
Numbers have kept him in debt for the
sake of 24% interest. The world has
too many formulas for a tender man.

He shares his last beer with my brother
on Boxing Day. Their delight in each
other warms me, a tenderness no technology
can reproduce. But I see too the flaw in
all that and where I went wrong, where I
have lost his acceptance of an imperfect world.
I want to know what fear is to a 66-year-old father.
I know he is a gentle man, one I cannot be.
Already, I have read too many words,
know too many formulas. With a head so full,
where is there room to start over,
to walk back into the house
and offer him my empty glass.

## *This Poem Will Not Harm You*

It contains only gentle words.
There are not death squads
waiting to claim you between
the syllables. The sounds of
explosions and death are faint
and belong to someone else's
composition. You can travel
safely here. It is quiet; rest
between the despair and loss.
Flowers grow carefully in this
poem. Their scents linger
through the rhythm of the
words. Turn each page lightly.
Surrender only as your tongue
imagines its taste. This poem
conquers nothing. Attacks
nothing. It shrinks from
aggression, from arguments,
jagged voices. Turn the page
lightly. Streets in this poem
are filled with music. Even the
dead are light; floating
without the familiar failure
of the grave. Turn the page
lightly. When you finish this
poem, sleep; think only of gods
and what you would like to ask
them. This poem holds no claim
on you, but release it gently.
Others have been tortured for

such thoughts. This poem doesn't care
about the colour of your skin or what
personal atrocities you have witnessed.
Release it gently. It belongs to
you now. There is one final image.
Read it aloud.
One letter at a time.

*Finding the Lights On*

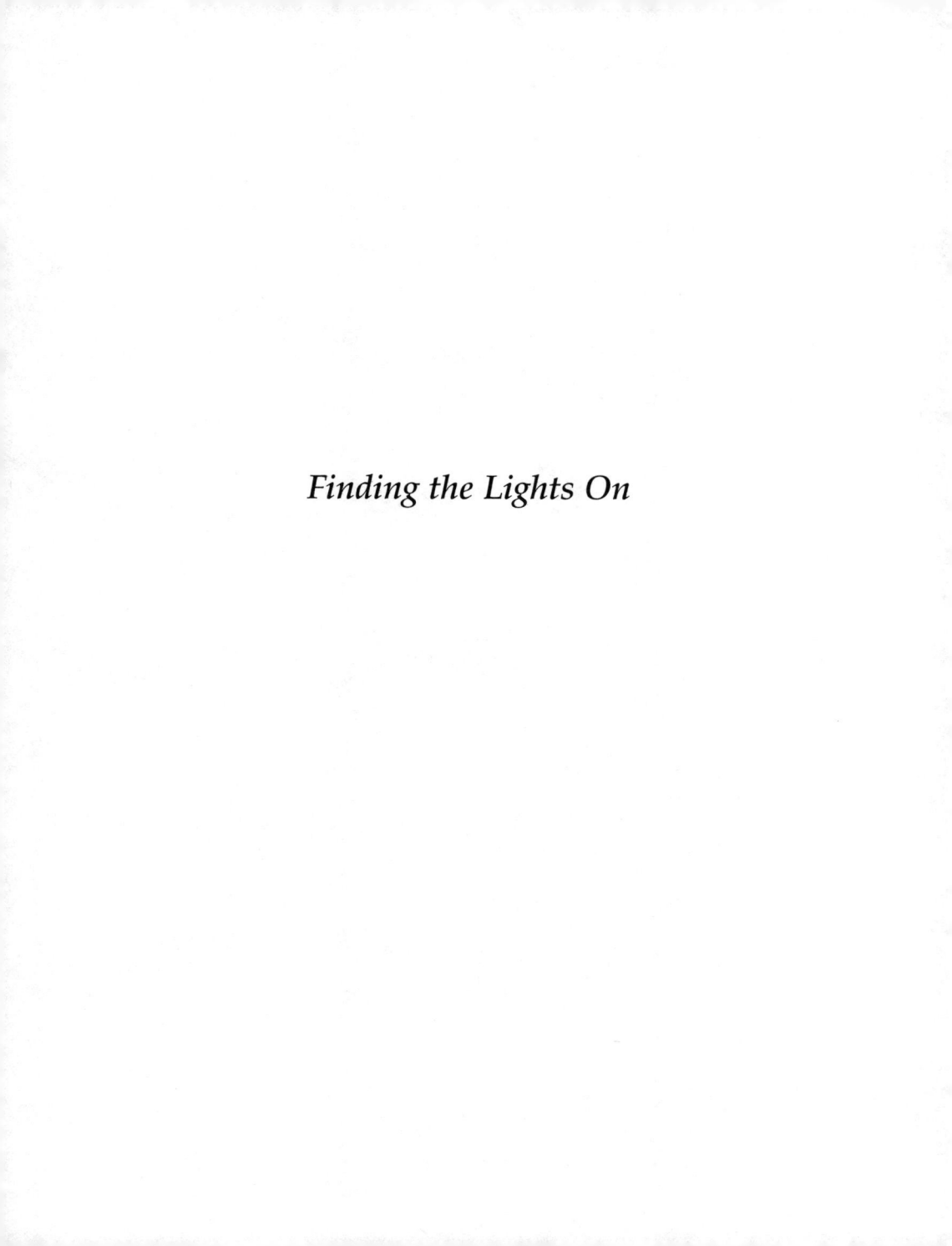

## Letters to My Mother

*Letter VIII*

The first separation was the hardest: son from mother. Suddenly two fleshes, not one. The others started when I was eight. The first time you ran away cursing Dad for the voices in your head. We ended up at the Salvation Army and I hated them because they did not understand your words, did not see that you were my mother and it was okay for you to rant on as long as you were there. They didn't know the isolation you had suffered, alone with no friends, hiding in the bush.

Eventually the police took you away in a small brown car. I cried. I hated my father too, could not face his gentle confusion. He shook inside, but I couldn't see it. Could only see your face in the car window looking back as though your life were disappearing into the eyes of your children. My brother, too young to understand, waved as if you were going on a visit to your sisters.

At the Salvation Army my sister, who was only a year old, needed a bottle and they warmed one for her while you sat in a ball crying, calling out God and Satan's names as though they were your children's names. I could hear the minister talking to my father on the phone, and I hated everyone except you. Your tears seemed to be the world. Turned away from me, you cried and I knew helplessness.

I wanted you to stop talking to yourself, so you could come home. But you didn't. They sent you to the Lakehead and your letters grew shorter and shorter. The voices never appeared in your letters, but they have never stopped. Even now when you visit I hear them late at night. Just faint whispers trailing off into sleep. And the rage grows on in me. Looking out a window and remembering those days makes me shudder and even the brightest day seems like a darkness. Both of us have been battered along the way not sure how two bodies start as one. Life is a separation. Letters intensify it, put words to the shadows that pass in front of us. Still we write because that is how we can react safely and still cope with the visits. Faces in photographs shrink.

*Letter XII*

You withdrew slowly, turning away with a smile as the sun passed suddenly like a scream. I couldn't see you breaking. Just one morning you were ironing and then you collected your three children as though they had to be shielded from what only you could see. On the highway, you flagged down a blue car and huddled near the door cursing while the driver tried to make small talk. I couldn't open my mouth, couldn't address his attempts to be polite. My lips trembled and I turned toward the passing landscape, usually familiar and safe but now transformed into an anguished blur. It wasn't you I turned to or my torn father standing at the curb in shock, it was the sky with its grey face at the car window. I tried to open the window but couldn't. My brother and I did not speak, stared straight ahead, tried to figure out if it was a nightmare or not.

Dad followed us into town in his 51 Ford. Later at the court house he and the doctor spoke in whispers. I felt the world explode with their delicate murmurs. I wanted them to tell me what to do, how to choose, as though my whole life depended on what I did next. You spoke and I tried to believe your words, see my father's face the way you described it. However, all I could do was bend with this new world, accept its twisted smile. That morning I was born, oldest son trying to forge it all back together. Going home in an April rain while my mother wrestled with God in a jail cell. My father unable to face himself in the mirror to shave. I couldn't speak to him, hated the doctor's perfect calm as he led us away from the court house. You standing at the curb, hands cuffed not seeing me disappear from your life as though I were never born. Sometimes later you would deny that I was your son would lie softly and claim that God was your husband, and you were here to watch over us because our real mother had run away. And I was scared that maybe it was true, that maybe I would never be born, that I could never be anyone's son again. Dad would not speak but faces the world since as if it were trying to tear out his guts.

Down the street an elderly woman sells boxes of oranges in January, and I am tempted to buy one and peel each orange to determine the degree of ripeness, to find the seeds that will not go away, that surrounded by all that flesh will still not flourish, but end as garbage. All day I think of nothing but oranges, see them in the windows, replacing the sun.

## *So Distant, So Near*

I hold you to protect you from harm
for a few minutes after the alarm.
Morning full of our bodies
the scent of last night's rain
passes quickly through the room.
I rise out of bed ready for work
uncertain of the ways I have hurt
you. Leave you still asleep,
covers at the foot of the bed in a heap.

In traffic, I forget the sink that won't drain,
the visitors that arrived last night.
The weather doesn't help with its endless rain.
During the night your moans gave me a fright.
Your tongue so smooth and sudden in my ear,
Morning so distant and so near.

## *To You*

When I am home alone, I feel I can talk to you.
Out shopping you don't care if I approve
don't care if I watch you or like the way you move.
You pose for a mirror thinking of me, too.
A small hat on your head, the sales clerk reminds
you of your mother. It is alone that I find

you. Your voice echoes pleasantly inside me
your hair with a touch of silver lies across my arm.
Your freckles fading the nearer you are and we
are different together, nothing left we can harm.
When I hear you at the door, I hide for a moment, afraid
that it is not you at the door, but someone I've made.

## A Gust Inside A God

*Rilke*

Why do I think of god as a wind
at all since his green face is no different
from mine or yours. His arms not a limb
from a tree, his back not bent,

His fingers not severed by a lover's teeth.
God is not a man with better clothes or a woman
who knows that her hands are trembling beneath
a yellow coat. Yet I look for her omens

On every street, look for her eyes in a store window
listen for her breath at night near my ear.
I listen for a wind that builds all night to crescendo.
God knows what I anticipate, what I fear.
Without some calming finale perhaps I would no longer
believe in what she does to my sleep at night
or that each day begins with a fright,
God nothing but a sighing that gets stronger.

## *Playing Music*

Do you feel the music slowly work its
way through your head until even your mouth
is swollen with it? It wakes you quick
from your dreams before completion. Without
music you never sleep for that long,
always dreading morning's slow explosion.
Some days you wake with a song
in your head you haven't heard before

Playing itself even still
deeper into your life. Notes spill
into your conversations. Followed by music
you can only listen, sway, and feel sick.
With each note your life unravels and as you fear
is lost forever in someone else's ear.

## Boy In A Choir

It's not murder that brings him to this church. He wants to feel God's affection while standing on a wooden bench. Sometimes God is late, too, not arriving until the choir is nearly finished practicing for the day. Late or not, God is welcomed. The boy can see that God has stopped being holy years ago, that he listens to the conversations of sinners because he is more interested in the gossip than in salvation. Still he remains loyal to those he has abandoned. Even his clothes reflect neglect: his shoes worn through. The boy has heard lovers tiptoe from his mother's room at night and each of them walks like God, the slow and natural walk of a man satisfied in love. Leaving the choir practice each Sunday, the boy pauses near the grave of his father. He listens for a sound, any sound, but all he ever hears is the music of the children in the nearby playground. Still their music is so beautiful he wants to dance in someone's arms. The boy is not disappointed that God can bring little more than sleep to our lives. But when the boy sings in the church beside other boys and girls, he can feel his mother's arms around her lover slowly slacken, can see her turn to look out a window at the Sunday traffic. Nearly on tiptoes the boy reaches for the highest note in a hymn, and as he does God slips out the side entrance and heads for the boy's house.

## *God's Moustache*

God is the last voice we hear at night as he practices his lines. When we finally see him it will not be his moustache that bothers us but his bent over posture. Light a cigarette I say and lean against your reflection in the mirror. God has no time to make order out of our chaos. He has no time to listen while we lie to one another about love. He is careful to ignore our mistakes to laugh when we call him divine. He is sympathetic but strong. When he is certain he will summon the wind and carefully he will form our words with it. Seeing us run, he will know that infinity is lonelier than he thought. When the wind finally lifts him above our trembling voices he will number the universe for us tossing bones at us to indicate the beauty he sees in us. There is no name he will take or certain path he will follow, his time amongst us exhausted before we understand that power begins with forgetting.

*A Breath at a Time*

## *The Numbers Begin*

The numbers begin
as a leaf folded
the break and crack of seams
the point where a tiny membrane
of light emerges
from heavy darkness
an image lost and rediscovered

the weight of things
gets in the way
the tension of smile laid upon smile
of paper towered on paper
the power of things
holding

## *A Breath At A Time*

We await the grace of dawn
the patient return of life

we hunger for
the voice of the voice

we dream without the presence
of memories

we wake up with hands
too large to be our own

we believe each whole sound
is the world

a breath at a time

## *So Holy Is The Mystery*

We make love because somewhere
apples are growing

I believe in the nights
we are magnificent
   together
when nothing can falter
   not even the music
that lifts from our bodies
forming a temple around us

I believe too in the times
   we are separate
when there is no music
   nor sacred thing to hold
delicately in our lips

we have so little time to form
   our stories
we have so many faces
   the mirror fails to
find the correct one

power is what cannot be explained
   music is the force
that draws out the folded links
   the sacred is silent
and necessary inside us
a mist envelops the hills and
I am nothing if I deny that

## *Nothing Is More Temporary*

Nothing is more temporary
than the words I use
to describe the way my heart
bends toward your heart

if I forget you for a moment
it is because I am filled
in infinite ways by your walk
or by how you slip out of bed
to find a cigarette

we are temporary and yet
we are filled by the permanence
of something beyond the utterable
it is caught in how you
strike a match
I see you eating strawberries
the folding together of red and pink
how lush this life is
and so minute each gesture
takes a lifetime to express

once I would have touched you
to convince you of my tenderness
now I touch you to learn
what tenderness is

## *Dead Eyes*

Under the water eyes are dead
darkness mars the light
only those without eyes can see
but above the surface of the lake
as the light fades we paddle a canoe
the miracle is in the rhythm
how one hand knows where the other one is
how the loon in an old costume
continues to call to ghosts
Keats would not understand this lake
and how under the water
there is a new death

the lake cannot be reached
its shore recedes toward the sky
and the longing continues
we are the images we believe
like the sun
we chase ourselves
until there is no one to catch

## *God*

God waits on street corners
for the famous to smile at him
He is invisible
even to His own mirrors
I praise His humble attempt
to expand our wonder

we fish in streams
to rehearse our deaths
we try to love one another
to free us from desire
God shaped trumpets for us
so that we could sing
through our skin

with our small hands
we expect to carve gods out of wood
we drive home alone in the rain
and look for a sign
as though God could be so creative
we look for answers with questions
and believe we can control things
by learning how they work

*Cantos From A Small Room*

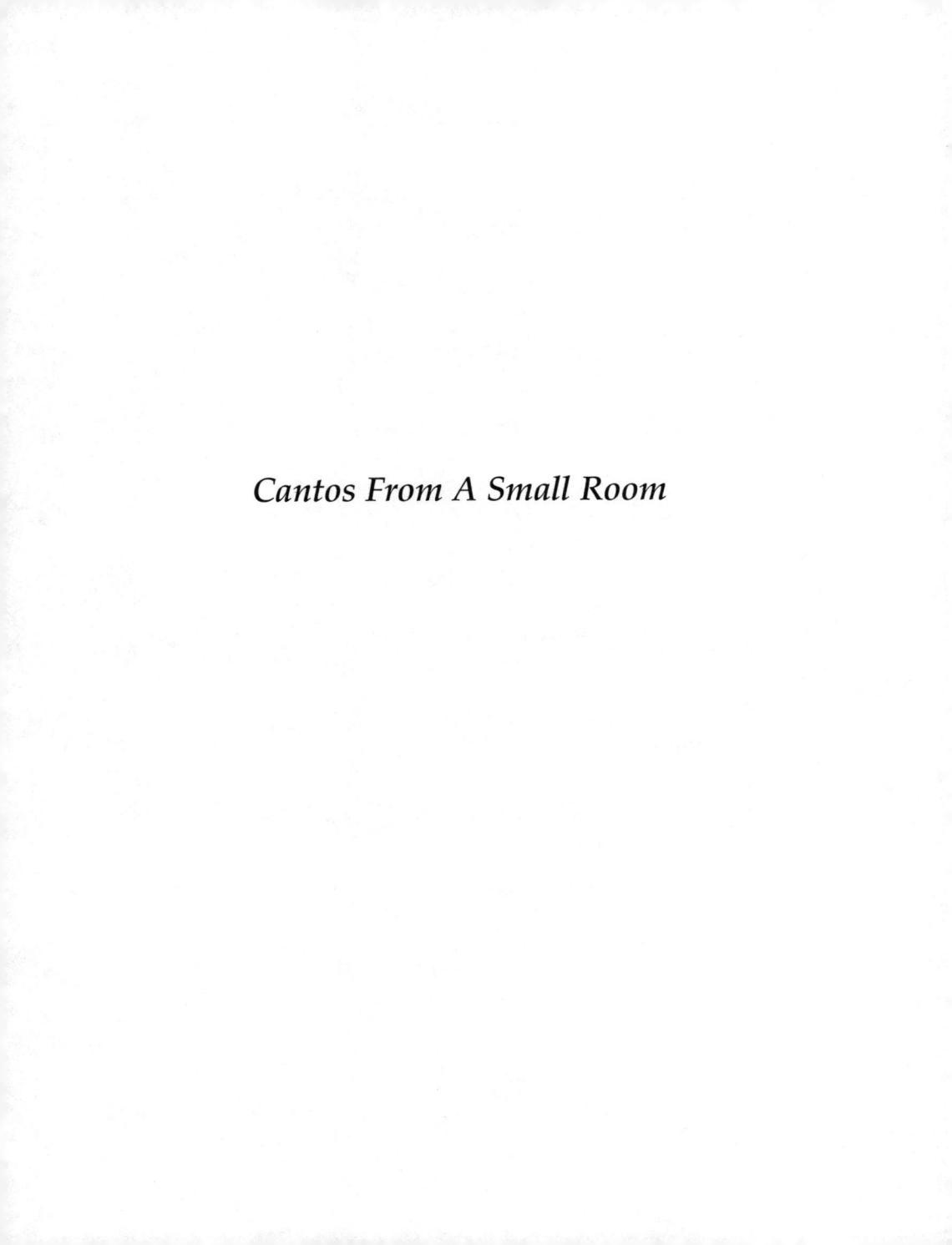

## *Canto 2: A Sigh A Petal Makes*

A sigh a petal makes as it falls, she made
and then nothing more. I remember
her words now. "I will not grow old except in the
memories of those who have stopped looking for me."
For months she knew it would happen and the
three of us would sit and drink tea and death
joined us and we were shy at first looking
into magazines for the faces of young women.
Still she remained defiant lifting her eyes
as she spoke. I was awkward more awkward than
either of you and I would kiss her
as she left and her warm lips healed my blunders.

There are a lot of words I want to leave out
place blank spaces here and there so that
others will know that there is too much I don't
know that her death fills every corner of my life
and each day I think of her barren form
left for the flames as we walked down the street
numb. Earlier she would visit us bring roses
and a book she just finished. Some nights
I hold my head in my hands for hours and I feel
as though I am walking down empty streets
while everyone else is asleep. Through it all
the chemotherapy, the hair falling out and growing back,
she would smile, light a cigarette and ask me
about my day as if I were the one who was
dying. Later in that room with a five
on the door she would do the same and then point to
the shelf on the wall where she had placed some toy
for Breanne. As I would turn to reach for it I could

feel her eyes close behind me and I would stand there
unsure that I could make them open again. I tried to say
something, anything that would drag her back into
this room to make her see the pale glory of the light
from outside as it bounced off two grey buildings
to reach here. I remember her at Christmas drinking wine
and once in a while rising so slowly to go to the bathroom.
I listened to her read to Breanne
and from those words and her voice I learned
that each of us faces death alone not able to let
others near enough to grab hold of our passing.
Today Rebecca is over packing her mother's things
and I write this unable to stop her words
from entering into my head as I try to trace
her passing with just a photograph and a keyboard.
It has rained nearly every day since she died.
This morning I awoke and the house was empty
and for a short time I imagined that this body I prepare
for death is younger and passing mirrors I forget that
somewhere behind me a crowd is gathering to break in.

## Canto 7: There Are No Accidents Between Lovers

I turned away and did not speak but
listened to your voice waver as
your mother's final breath passed.
We waited all day knowing it would be
soon tomorrow or the day after but soon
and still it was too quick as if suddenly
a switch had been thrown somewhere.
Both of us wanted her to stand up and walk over
to where we were sitting and put her
arms around us as she has often done
in the past. But we knew that the past
is a fragrance that could not reach into her room.
Looking at her closed eyes I wondered if
where she dreamed there was
a bird singing outside her window.
After she died, I gripped your hand and
saw that in death even music falters.

I cannot forget her final breath
that last moment so quiet it
passed unnoticed by everyone there.
We were all talking and did not hear.
We felt helpless and turned to the window
hoping to see her face but there was
nothing but a sky filled with sunset.
The world outside so quiet it was deafening.
I did not know that death would be so quiet
a pause that most alive do not hear
their ears listening too hard for something else.

She did not open her eyes or sit
up suddenly and point at anyone just
stopped breathing. None of her
sweet laughs we used to wake to
when we lived in her house, none
of the wide smiles as she bent
to lift Breanne, her granddaughter.
That is what makes it so hard
the memories that linger even now
months later summer all around us.

Some nights I talk to her as you sleep
and I know that sorrow is a thing
that continues long after the world
has grown up around the absence.
We fill each day as we can forgetting
her phone number or never driving by her house
as we once did to see if she was home.
Staring at her picture in the hall trying
to remember the sound of her voice.
Everyone else in the pictures fades until
all we can see is her staring out
at the camera as if she were in a
foreign country and wasn't
sure of the customs.
Sometimes her name pops into my head
and I say it over and over afraid
I might forget how I would call to her
from the living room at her house as
she knelt outside in the flower bed
planting things I still can't name.

When we speak of her our voices pause.
We know that there is a losing
side to love and even after she is gone
we go on loving her while we learn
to live in new ways waiting at Christmas
for her piano playing even though
her piano is at our house now and
sits silent as if it has forgotten its music.
As I pass it each day in the hall,
I think of our lovemaking and of your
mother alone moving through the thoughts
of so many each day but soundless
faint like her final breath
implanted on so many.
Some nights I stand recklessly in the rain
and feel my life leaving and coming
back to me each moment and as I stare
I see how the world opens around my place in it.
Like everyone else, I am tied not to the sun
or moon or the voices I shape each day
but to this faint breath in my chest
moving softly to my mouth and out
noticeable to you only as I sleep.

## Canto 9: The Dream Canto

Seeing you in your coffin makes me want to
wake you and make death return another
day when crocuses are not blooming on the
hills behind the house. The bruise on your
hand where the IV rested does not go away even
in death it lingers betraying the undertaker's
careful work. You do not smile or move even
though you would have liked to see the people
here. Instead all we can do is lay flowers and
read poems that slow us down and make us think
of your dust as it moves through a bed of roses
finding rest in the quiet earth. Your lips
are dry you hair softer but combed in a
way you would not have liked.

Each of us before your coffin listens
for a sigh to steal from your lips.
Your new silence does not seem right.
We do nothing but listen deeply to
your life pass through our heads.
We whisper the words you liked the most,
or think of the colours you thought of
when in pain or alone or sad.
We know the shape you formed around each
of us is gone and we look from one to another
like sleepers waking from a long dream.
In this room one of us thinks of the sea
and feels it pound the lava of the beach
then turn again into the sea
falling into its grave of water.

We have brought you flowers because they can
hear you better than we can as they burn with you.
Our eyes photograph all this and yet the
ceremony remains invisible.
Quietly, we alternate our fingers in another's grip
and grief does not leave us but takes us like fools out
into the sunlight. It was at sunset that you quietly
stopped breathing and those of us there
took hold of your hand or kissed your lips
as if a part of you could still be reached with such
efforts. We did not sing but wept and nothing passed
to us except the spring day we later poured out into
the sun's final rays blinding us.

We kissed each other because inside
there was nothing but light.
Your voice called softly from the hospital but we
could not hear it anymore could not
return to that room even the few minutes away changed
everything. Your body merely a husk now was not something
we could spend the night beside.
After days alone with you in that room
looking out toward the mountains and the half block
to your house, we cannot go back.

After the service we linger in front of the
funeral home no longer sure how to stand or speak.
We avoid talking about your death coming so soon
in your 57th year. Earlier you daughters
couldn't stop kissing you. Each bent to your brow
awkwardly not the way they would have if you
were still alive. You would have liked that kissing
by each of your daughters just as they were made with
your flesh and love and you held them fresh from your body.

Now they stand before your coffin and know it is not you
that they see. Death completes nothing
and as I bend to your face I see that what you have
left for us is not this shell but the dreams around it.
As I kiss you this last time, there are no eyes
to open to nothing but the smells the undertaker
could not take out and that bruise on your hand where
the IV was for days. You do not speak as we part
as you once would have. No all your words are lost
except those you left behind folded into notebooks.
Scribbled in your quick hand. They do not tell us
how to bring you back. We read them to each other
to hear again your voice part the darkness.

## *Map Of Light*

We begin the journey the same, travellers
hurled together at great speed. Impacting
on a single point of light.
We exist because there is a certain tension
between particles, because somewhere
a blue light is twisted into red, because
at an intersection four cars stop simultaneously.
The radio drums in our ears like the confused
beating of a raven's wings. The light is green
through the window this morning and I try to
lift your face above me but in your eyes
the light is red. What are those bells you ask
and I listen but there is nothing except a
clock ticking and the cat downstairs somewhere
skinning a mouse. There are stars in your eyes
and I move closer to count them. We have accepted
the convenience of our bodies and have learned
how they can fill with passion. The children
we form are part of our shared breath, part
of the moon through the skylight.

Today we put up the Christmas tree and the ornaments
we unpack add shape to the past we carry inside.
We can't find the angel. Somehow it got lost
when we moved. Instead, we buy a new one.
I find your mouth over me warming the air
with your breath. You move slowly searching
for a way inside my head, to reach the places
where the light is taken over by night.
Inside me, you dance as though my darkness

formed the sweetest music. As I close
my eyes I can follow your movements feel
your dance far inside me and for hours
later I can't let the light out,
can't stop feeling your movements.
You need no map to find the light in me.
I wish we could fold back the darkness
for good, stop our faces from being defeated
by the light, by the days we sit alone
afraid of the mirror, afraid of the way
our faces are wearing out.
We make love at night, listen as a train
passes and we feel as though we were on it.

We fit together, not sure why or how
we only know that we do. No one is singing
as we turn out the lights for sleep.
Above us the moon waits as though
it could feel our longing. I turn to you
our lips meeting softly in the dark.
We are wrapped within again. Loving
the quiet, the softness of one another.
Later as you sleep I think of the thousand
different ways we could have arrived at this
moment. I am amazed that we fit as we do,
the light in this room is always white
clear as though here at the top of our house
we have found an atmosphere that lets our longing open.
Light searching inside for the darkness
that has been there the longest.

*88*

## *Meandering*

We look for evil in what a god does.
It is only through us
that gods know a false thing.
But gods are false too.
We find in their chest a cavity
we fill with mirrors and with thoughts
we don't mean.

Today the buses are on strike and it
is too cold to venture out.
Stranded I take my arm from the windowsill.
My head is as big as a god's
and yet it is filled with a single thought
one I can't get rid of. It remains
even as I walk into the cold.
This thought grows into madness
or evil and I am a fool because I chose
it and now it fills everything
I find in my body's own truth.

Gods are numbers safe in our minds.
Not plucked from the sky at all
nor more certain than we about how to talk
to a lover. Inside our mothers
we form our bodies from a blueprint
they pass delicately to us
in their blood. After birth
we learn the parts of ourselves that
are the least god-like. Those features
we have no say over but bear until death.
Everything came true as we lived it
our lives bound by a brutality
we hardly recognized in others.

Life is an orchestra unwrapping its music
without the interference of an conductor.
I see too that the good is good whether
it is named or not. Evil is what
proclaims the false as true.
My own fingers on your
thigh is proof that I am wrong.

## *God Is The Smallest Object*

God is the smallest object in a room. Some of us see it and speak to it as if it were a pet or a lover. Others imagine it was bigger and could not fit into this room at all. Others still fall in love with it and take it to bed with them every night. Some of us can't even get into the room at all and must stare at the object from the doorway like a prisoner staring at the sea from their cell window. This object does not move or breathe or even love. It merely thinks about ways to get out of this room for good. It thinks about wings about legs about fingers but none of them is adequate. In the end this object decides that it is stuck in this room for good. Those that truly love it will pick it up and throw it out the window. Those who despise it will try to hide it beneath some large piece of furniture. Most of us, however, will take no notice of it merely sit next to it once in a while and glance at if from the corner of our eyes hoping that sometime we will discover what to do with it.

*Nothing Vanishes*

## *Nothing Vanishes*

### 1

My mother picks mushrooms
out in the bush, small hands
reaching between the thistles
perfectly, never once getting
nicked. She doesn't worry about
picking poisonous ones.
She knows what they look like
and avoids them.
Her fingers, smelling musty
from all those mushrooms,
reach up from the earth
to touch me.

Mushrooms line the table
and she cuts through some
and washes others and she
offers me one and I look at it
for awhile and then
put it in my mouth,
never sure if it is poisonous or not.
Her fingers have remained young
despite everything.
As she cleans the dirt from
beneath a nail later,
she sings softly to herself.
I want to join in but don't,
just listen as the past lingers
outside every window and all
I can taste is mushrooms for hours after.

2

She boils rice on the wood stove
and fries some of the mushrooms
and tastes one now and then.
She doesn't care what I'm thinking
or what the fire begs her to do.
She ignores everything but her cooking—
the mushrooms pulled quickly, authoritatively
from the stove.

After supper my mother
puts the rest of the mushrooms
in the fridge hiding them
in various brown paper bags.
Tomorrow after I return to the city
she will continue to eat them,
looking at them on her plate,
gentle reassuring shapes.
For a moment they might look
ruined, all shrivelled there
waiting to be consumed,
becoming once more what the earth
expected. And as she eats them,
somewhere inside her she
loses and finds again her God.
Her soul is something she thinks of
as she looks at her young fingers.
Her son so far away calls to ask
about the mushrooms, but doesn't,
asking about something else instead.

3

New mushrooms come up to replace
the ones she picks.
In a few weeks she will go out
to collect them, returning
to familiar rocks and trees.
Sometimes while picking mushrooms
she will kneel to pray,
the bush so quiet her heart
forms a thunder around her.
I can almost hear her prayers
as I imagine her kneeling before
a certain pine tree.
Its not the words I hear
but the murmurs between each word,
long and certain coming from
where I imagine her soul to be.
When she stands again her legs are shaky
and I reach out a hand to steady her
but touch the window of my office
instead. Opening my eyes
the city looks aimless as it
vanishes at the horizon.
The earth beneath her feet
supports her as my outstretched hand can not.

4

I don't buy mushrooms in the supermarket
but walk past them and see my mother
turning her nose up at them,
tame and small on the counter.
She is what I will dissolve into.
I am what she has left the world
and my skin no different than hers
washes in the sunlight and does not
shine but reflects a dull image
of something bright.

5

I do not send her flowers or telegrams
just show up now and then,
expecting to eat mushrooms
and to talk.
When my plate is empty
I will lay down my knife and fork
knowing that when God comes
he can do no damage
or provide any answers,
because the only answers there are
I have already found:
my stomach full, the night
still a few hours off,
and my mother moving about
her small house as if
she were already in heaven.

## *Speaking In Tongues*

I undress and you
lie on the bed with
your hands open
giving me something
to taste on your palm.
Your eyes are closed,
the skylight hums with light.
I close my eyes and see you
as still as the living can be.
I begin to dance for you
first my fingers then arms then all
of me and you answer back
move for move and then I answer
you and we sweat together
old and young at the same time
saved by orgasms
from growing cold.
I speak in tongues for you
moving my mouth to where
you call me and alone
like this we claim each
our own pleasure.
Our lovemaking
without opposites
no longer man and woman
using murmurs instead of words.
Signals learned from the beginning
of the world learned
and let out when together
speaking in tongues until
morning fits around us like a new skin.

*Chances*

Chances are that we will
grow weary in the evening's chill.
Holding hands we can warm
each other while infinity

looms in both directions.
Our noses find the scent
the gods left us to follow.
Lying in the grass

we let the stars
hypnotize us.
And we hold fast

until we are sure
we won't clutter the sky
with our flight

## Waiting In The Dark

I remember getting off the school bus
on a cold night in February not wanting
to look up the road, afraid the lights
might not be on and the dark empty house
invisible at the end of the road.
Later I made the fire in the wood stove
as my younger brother collected wood.
Dad was in town somewhere drinking, forgetting about
supper and the two boys who waited alone ten miles
in the bush. Their mother 300 miles away
in a mental hospital. I waited with my brother
in front of a grey TV screen watching
Ben Casey and the crazy way it began: Man, Woman, Infinity.
The word Infinity sounded as cold as
the face of the window behind my neck. The faint glow
of the dangling light bulb was the only finite thing left.
I could not go to the window could not look out
into the snow to watch for the headlights of Dad's truck.
As I remember now, I think not of the cold or the waiting
but of the darkness broken occasionally
by the flash of headlights on the Trans Canada.
I think of being just nine years old
and learning that the darkness stays inside and lingers
even on the nights when I found the lights on,
Dad waiting, eyes sore from crying
or being alone too long in front of the TV.
Unemployed, he watched the days pass as though
he was shut out forever. He didn't know how a lover's hand
passes in a dream like a kiss or a threat. His wife
300 hundred miles away. He gave up fighting

long ago waiting for me to come home,
an uncomfortable father no longer sure
what the right thing is or what is
noble or good. He had no one to blame.
Even God was a fake
who concealed himself with a beard
or mumbled to those who hid behind
the closed door of a church.
Dad would wait for me to make supper.
I would open cans and toss their contents
into boiling water, turning away to find a window,
any window.

Some winter nights now when I am the first one home,
I enter the empty house expecting to find
my father standing in the dark
whispering to me.
In the corner my mother stands
smiling as though dreaming someone's caress.
I can't forget, can't stop running around
the house turning on lights, pulling down blinds.
Those dark arrivals all those years ago taught me
how we are slowly broken, our parents
just as out of control as we are. Their faces
accepting gestures or expressions that the nerves
created on their own. Impulsively they smile as a child
walks toward them for the first time.
Our minds are sometimes like jelly that bounces around
in our skulls gently bending to fit
the bone structure that contains them.
Each of us stands in a dark doorway
but only those around us see the doorway
or the darkness behind us.

Still I, like others, listen to more stories
as though waiting for an explanation or solution
that will hold me together as I stand
in front of a dark house alone. Inside it
my whole life is pinned to the walls waiting
in its own darkness, in the cold infinity
that surrounds it all the time I am away.

## *Apples*

Apples fall to the ground and the boy fills a sack with them and drags it to where his father stands smiling as if life held only mysteries like this. Someday the boy may be a soldier and may die a great distance from this apple tree. The man will already be dead and will never know how his son falls. Now each takes a bite from a different apple and watches the other chewing as if an apple's sweetness could be seen in another's face.

The boy would rather be playing with his friends or in his room, but he likes to feel the apple's flesh swell in his mouth. When he is a soldier, he will think about this day many times, remembering the shape of the apple as it filled his hand. Even when he hoists his gun in the heat of battle and squeezes the trigger, he will imagine that he is holding an apple. But when he dies he will be thinking of something different as the apple in his throat swells until no more air can get around it.

The boy took the sack of apples into his mother. She will can some of the apples and make pies with others. Later in the kitchen, the boy watched his father wash his hands and turn with them, still damp, to his wife, to kiss her cheek. The boy put one of his fingers in his mouth and it tasted of dirt and apples. As he stood there sucking his finger, his throat began to lose its dryness and his life continued around him and he felt like an apple on a giant tree waiting to ripen. His father passed him, carrying the empty sack back to the yard. The father stood below the empty tree asking himself something that the boy would never hear.

*Tomatoes*

You sent me out for tomatoes
and at a stoplight
I picked a tomato from the bag.
I wanted to bite
into the tomato
but didn't, thinking
of your hand running
down my back, your tongue
moving between my legs.
It was at sunset and the sky
listened to my breathing,
a few pink clouds
soothing on the horizon.

At the door you didn't take
the tomatoes but took
my lips instead,
covering them with your own,
your tongue filling
every place in my mouth.
We followed the remaining lights upstairs.
Our footsteps were
without echoes.

I had learned how to slow
my fingers down, how
your breathing carries guidance.
Over me you were slow and
certain, filling me
with a gracefulness
old bones master reluctantly.

The room, the city, the world
didn't hear us as
your hands followed my thoughts.
Your body lead my hands
as they lifted
your thighs toward my mouth.
I sang into you
uttering something from the back
of my throat.
We didn't stop, just slowed down.
My hands washed you down
with your sweat.

In the morning I open a window
taking a fresh breath
of cold winter air
cooling what still smoulders.

I find the bag of tomatoes
at the front door, hidden
partially by the morning shadows,
sitting so quiet like a promise.
I leave them there and wait
for you to discover them,
to lift one to your mouth,
your fingers slowly
covered with juice.

## Last Words To A Father

There can be none, only a short wave or certain smile that comes again when you are asleep or talking to your daughter, her head tossed a particular way as if she were trying to figure you out. On some Saturday or Sunday you will call home and there will be no answer only a long ringing in your ear, and as you put down the receiver the words will form again at the back of your mind, and you will think of a particular color or taste, and you will open your mouth as if to speak but you will step forward instead and look into your hands as if they held something beautiful, and as you do you will begin to cry, and from across the room a thin pale smoke will drift as if your father has just finished smoking one of his strong cigarettes. You will stare at the empty chair. The house quiet on a quiet street. Off in the distance a dog will bark at someone. The world will become so faint that you will begin to see behind it the face of your father and his eyes. How did they get there?

*Breathing Distance*

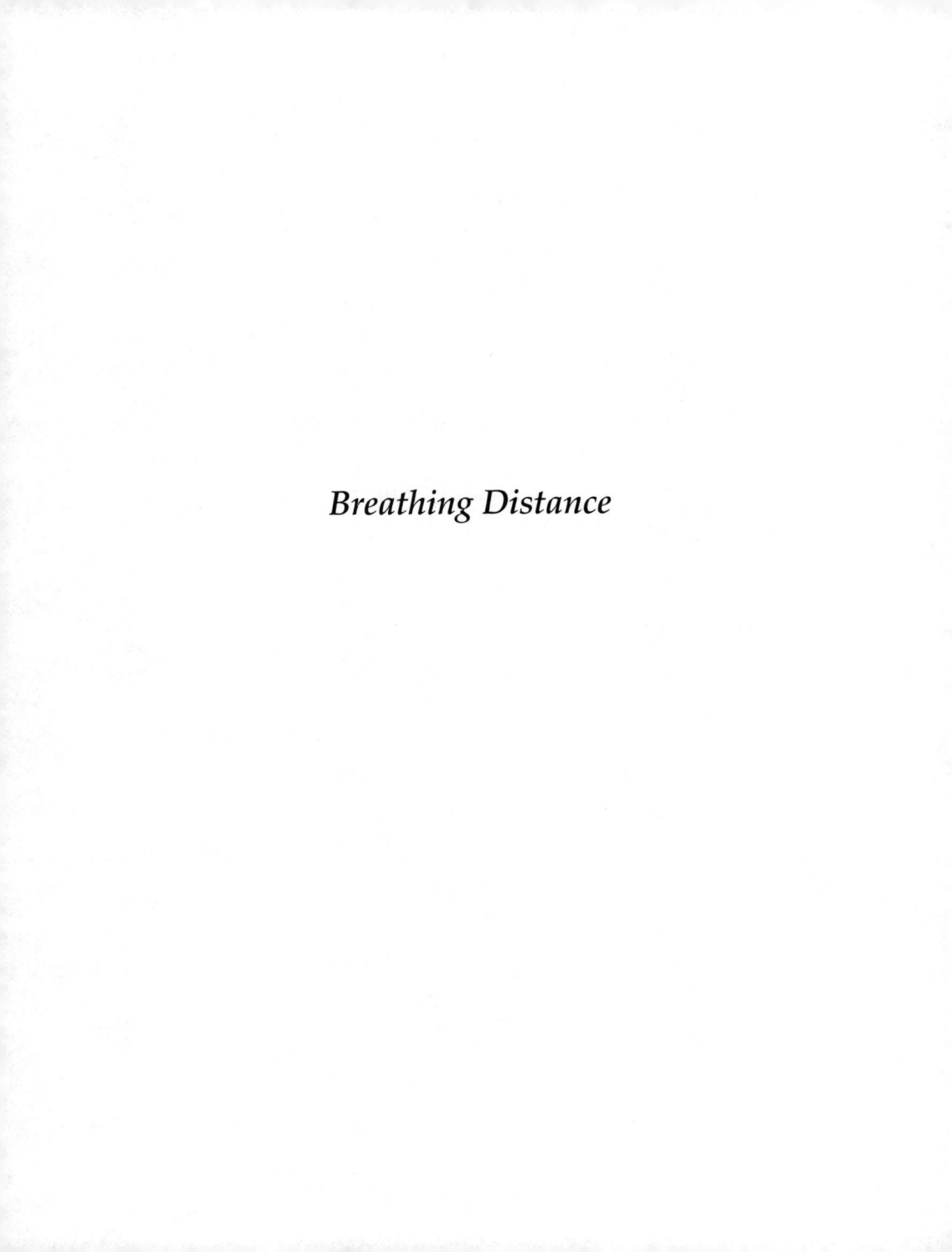

## *Ode To Isaac Babel And My Dead Father*
### *for August 27, 1920*

On the morning my father was born, Isaac Babel left Sokal in Poland on route to Laszczow with the Red Army. The Bug River could have flowed red that day but was mud brown as the warring army moved further west dragging the border of Poland with them. Sokal is now on the border of the Ukaraine though it was the middle of Poland then. The Polish troops made it as far as Minsk, but were turned back. My father slipped from his mother as if coming out of hiding and the light was so brash it made his mother invisible to him. In that great white the world throbbed as if it were adding the pain of Poland to my father's. Soon his mother vanished from his life for good.

That first night of my father's life, Isaac Babel wrote in his notebook about a normal day, for war too becomes ordinary piloted more by the odd shifts of the sky than anything human. The next day, my father's first full day alive, Babel describes the slaughter of Jews by retreating Poles in a village and he knows the Cossacks he rides with are no better than those Poles. My father slept by his mother for a few hours before the nurse carried him, wrapped tightly, back to the nursery at the St. Joseph's hospital in Kenora. She let him slip gently from her arms into the waiting crib his eyes opening and closing wildly on his new world. I can see his face in my mind, his infant eyes trying to see through the blur. Perhaps the nurse already knew his fate and urged a little extra care on him. I imagine his unwed mother slipping out that second day heading back east with her father, but she must have stayed longer while her body healed. She came back to him in dreams at the end of his life as death waited as if a dark promise from her red lips. I wonder what she whispered to my father those few early hours of his life. Did some echo of it lodge inside him for good? Perhaps our infant selves know the darkest secrets given us when the world is still so vast it has no shape.

The second night of my father's life, Isaac Babel slept uneasily. The cruelties of war felt raw on his skin and made life hopeless. On the third day, my father's eager blue eyes opened hungry for the world. His mother was a warmth in the fog around him that he edged toward with hardly a sound. While Babel learned about revenge, my father learned about love and how all our earthly acts form pale shadows in a nearly dark room.

September 15, 1920 was the last entry in Babel's notebook. In it he makes a subtle attack on the Red Army and it is clear by now he hates his traveling companions. My father was less than a month old and he was already separated from his mother for life. He could see a little clearer by then, but his mother was already on the train back east to Cobalt. In 1939, Babel was shot for being silent too long, for silence worried Stalin the most. My father's quiet would have troubled Stalin too.

## *Ode To Sakutaro Hagiwara*

I walked the streets of your city, Maebashi,
looking for the bicycles of your poems
and for the moon you howled at
like a lover anxious for morning.
I do not know the Japan you lived in and
barely know the one I walk now its streets so
full of people it's hard to hold my place.
I want to see your city in winter the branches
bending beneath snow but must walk it
in late summer the heat soiling my clothes.
At the Museum of Literature I looked at your shoes
still curved to the shape of your feet
and your hats still remembering your head
as if it could come back to them.
Behind glass the things from your life seem
too personal and I want to look away
as if I've wandered into your bedroom by mistake
and yet I understand this need to save the past
and can imagine all the school children
who file past this display each year
learning that here is what a poet leaves behind
as well as the poems so right they changed modern
Japanese poetry forever. Your statue greets everyone
outside the museum and faces the Tone River,
a narrow, sculptured river that winds invisibly
through the downtown. Its banks have been carved
to make the river twist through the city
as though it were constructed along with the buildings.
Yet I felt at home here in this artificial place
because your statue kept poetry alive.

I reached into the chilling water of the Tone fed like the Bow
in Calgary by mountain water. I reached my hand in
to still the water but it moved rapidly over my hand ready
to take my hand with it if I could let it go.
Behind me your statue ached
and I turned my head several times
expecting you to walk up behind me and recite
a poem the water has inspired
all these days it has flowed in front of you.
And I expected the addicting moon.
I wanted you, or the river,
or even the moon to ask me to stay.
But I couldn't and when I turned around
the water did not stop nor did you move.
Neither you nor the river has a will
only a quiet obedience of the dead.
I walked off toward the busy street nearby
craving the purpose of the moving crowd
flowing from street to street like a living river.

## Ode To Tadeusz Rosewicz

*that old woman who*
*is leading a goat by a rope*
*is more necessary and more precious*
*than the seven wonders of the world*
*and anyone who thinks and feels*
*that she is not necessary*
*is a mass-murderer*
                    **Tadeusz Rosewicz**

I see that woman too and the children
she brought here hidden beneath her dress
to explain to them that the world
is wrought with pain and suffering
and too much is pried apart.

She dances as her body aches
and night is a dress she wants
to remove and place by the side of the bed
as one does before making love
and still no truth worth knowing
fails to replace evil.
The killing is done each moment
and as she leads the goat toward town
she could stop to let it feed but doesn't.
She talks to water and listens
to the sky for lost in its blue invitation
is all that has disappeared.
She could name those lost
or born to the world too soon
their eyes burned by cruel light.

When she stops at your house
to tell you about the goat
invite her in and tell her the names
of those you love and how
they wander in search of your love.
Tell her how winter stayed
too long this year and wore each of us
a little quicker toward death.
Sing for her and offer her a sweet farewell
as she ventures out into the street again
the goat walking behind her in defiance
his death already outside the poem
as is hers and yours only in the poem
is it unclear where she is going.

## Ode To Death

*Thou art a dreaming thing – John Keats*

I have been bothered all week
by dreams of my dead father.
Each time I wake
I feel lost in the light that scrambles
to make another day and I know
the dead come back to the living
not to tell them anything
but because they still know the way.

Each time I wake
I remember him in the hospital morgue.
His dead face could not answer me
and still I talked to him and kissed his forehead
as if my warm lips could reach him
hidden so deep within his body.
I wanted to sing a song
the room could hold in its thin air forever,
but the nurse made me feel
like his dead body belonged to everyone but me,
and I left ashamed that only the dead
have taught me about death
and even they could not explain
how I should love them.
Now when I wake it's my dead father's face
I remember even if he was alive in the dream.

My father will never see the green yards
in Calgary again or lift his hand
into the sunlight to strum its warmth.
The dead leave no trace to where they've gone
and in dreams the living mold
a different world
where death is but a window
the living can look into
and find across the glass
a world like this one,
a strange world and yet
one we can live in.

When I wake from a dream of my father
I wander the house
as if I've just come in the wrong door.
I approach his pictures
as I might someone living
and speak to them
expecting his head to nod and his eyes
to come back into focus.
But he doesn't move
remaining still as all ghosts do.
In my dreams and in my head
he remains alive
even if no one but me can see him
and though he doesn't move at all
we communicate through stillness
and within my worn out head
we dance without moving
to music nothing more than arteries' work
and the glorious confusion of love.

Spring bends inside me,
and my father can feel
a fresh green stretch out of me
can smell each flower's new bloom.
I carry spring for him
and when I sleep he seeks it out.
Even if the dead can't return
they do all the same
for the living light the way
with dreams.

*Somewhere Between Obstacles
And Pleasure*

## *Shaped By The Wind*

We drive north of Carbondale Lookout
and pass trees shaped by the prevailing wind.
Beneath the surface history grows
and the earth collects each thing that dies
willing to hold all that time has let loose.

Pine trees lean east as if in motion
caught mid flight like fleeing animals,
except, unlike us, trees and plants
are joined to the earth
by restless roots
grasping dark soil.

You drive briskly
and lean over to squeeze my knee.
You say *I love you,*
and I forget history boiling beneath us,
forget the birth of coal,
think only of your warm hand,
as it seeks
the soft spot above my knee
pushing gently
like a root taking hold.

## The Barking Dogs Of San Miguel II

### 1

They bark late into the night
no one to silence them
as they disturb our sleep.

I imagine no bones
beneath their fur,
no heart hidden in their chests,
nothing inside but pure spite.

During the day they appear lazy and docile
crossing streets in front of me
without a single bark.
They look harmless then
as if recently dropped,
homeless to move from street to street
too timid to even lift their heads
when they pass. Demure and restless
they never stay still for long,
but meet in open fields
to ply through garbage.

In the afternoon heat, they cower in shade
lifting a head now and then to let those passing
know they are still alive.
Some, brave or careless,
sleep in the middle of the street
and appear dead from a distance.

During the night no one opens a door or window
to try and quiet the noisy dogs
and when I ask about them
I'm told not to listen.
I wonder if Pearl and I are the only ones
listening as the dogs bark through the night.
I give in and wear ear plugs
slip my empty hands beneath the covers
and test along the length of myself
feeling the outline of various hidden bones.

What shudders in the dogs also shudders in me.
Still, I see their insides as bottomless,
washed clean by some scavenger logic.
I believe their tongues are connected to darkness.
Their barks drawn from airless insides.
They are the end of the world.
Guardians to what our boned world won't acknowledge.

There is no way to sleep,
no way to fathom how unhinged
their world is; next to ours,
but as invisible as the bottom of a deep well.
They will not quiet.
Their barks are aimed
beyond the rim of lights out to real darkness
where their souls got lost
a long time ago between sand and cactus,
left by mistake
for safe keeping.

2

There was a dead dog at the outskirts
of San Miguel that I passed every day
when I went for a walk.
Her life leaked out
until she swelled with death,
her brown fur turning red, then purple.
The smell made me turn back
but still I had to see
what changes each day brought.
On the last day,
her insides had exploded
through her cracked hide.
Birds circled above
and her entrails oozed,
fleeing her body
after having been held in so long.
Her eyes had been stolen
by one creature or another
and her tongue still touched the pavement
as though she were licking something there.
I turned back and saw San Miguel
spreading up over the hills
and I could hear from the distant streets
the odd bark of a dog.
I headed toward that sound
as if I was entering the city
for the very first time.

## *What Bodies Hold*

You have shown me how the moon catches fire as it touches the trees. You have taught me that we fit together even beneath bone and skin. In the dark of my head, I find you, and as we kiss, a warm shiver enters that dark and we each cross over gingerly, not knowing how dark the wind nor what the rain answers. You have helped me to laugh and to listen in the wind for the way home. I love how your laugh squeezes from the night a place to be happy. I love how you whisper softly in my ear. Even the sound of my name is new, trembled between lips and sighed to me in love. I answer your name back. There is nothing it doesn't mean.

## The Soul's Journey

### 1

The soul is what shivers in us,
what light seeks as it burrows inside.
The soul's journey is shapeless,
storyless, timeless,
unwarmed,
neither seamed nor seamless.
The soul simply passes this way,
whispers,
and then vanishes.

I forgot the soul
until I saw loved ones die,
their eyes open on a different world.
I called to them,
whispered in their dead ears
then I saw
what the soul leaves behind
empty, hard, nameless;
nothing more than
a flesh and bone museum.
Perhaps I should have opened a window
made the soul's path easier.
Instead, I sat on their beds and wept
the light rippling over my hands.

2

I look into your eyes
and see the little girl afraid,
stretching out in the dark
for something at the end of her bed.
And before that?
Were you who your mother expected
as she paced restlessly
looking now and then into the fridge,
your father coughing into his hands?
There must have been a moment
when she looked at you and was happy,
and he too, even if after a while they hardened
and could not be in the same room together.
You slipped from them
back into the dark shadow they stood against,
the day working hard to wear them out.
You're not the story they made
but the one you complete on your own.
You stand in the kitchen sipping iced tea
and I want to draw you so close
that when we kiss our souls will touch.
Your mother caught your soul for you
and housed it inside her
shaped it with your father's aid
and together they held you up to the light
gave you a name and then
let you slip away.
Now when the two of us are alone,
the children elsewhere,
I listen in the quiet of our house
for any sound your soul might make,

and in my thoughts
I see you walking between your parents,
your hands swallowed by theirs,
your shadow dragging behind you
following you everywhere
like it too wanted a heart,
and some mornings when I turn to you,
your eyes push open my heart,
and I know the souls inside us
record everything
and will carry it all away one day,
taking our love
beyond light's reach.

## *Heat Locked*

When I came in from a walk
the frying pan had overheated and
had become stuck to the burner.
Heat locked, you said later,
and I had to ask you again
not sure what you'd said.
I thought of the sun holding
the earth in place
and of the wood stove my mother
cooked over,
her hands warmed all day long.
Now she complains
her hands are always cold
as if she misses that stove.
I thought of the earth's core boiling
like a blast furnace,
a hot core that keeps us righted
whichever side of the planet we inhabit.
I thought of hot springs bubbling to the surface,
of heat drawn to cold out of love,
and of the woman in the Crowsnest Pass
who told us she could smell a Chinook
coming whenever she passed the site
of the old Turtle Mountain Hotel,
could smell it a full day before it arrived
a distinctly sulfurous odour
as the earth eagerly gives up its warmth.
I thought of when we kiss
and how our warm breath circles our mouths,
our lips joining us
with warm fissures.

I thought of how we think of ourselves
as warm creatures seeking fire
not pain, seeing the light not dark
and how as a boy I put my feet in the oven
to warm them and
how we lit fires in barrels
in the middle of frozen lakes
huddling in front of them
while our lines probed the dark water for fish.

I thought of all the candles we light
and how we sip wine and watch them flicker.
Sometimes I close my eyes
and wish on one
opening my eyes again
to its dome of heat
wanting to feel the warmth run along my skin,
wanting to see exactly where it opens me and enters.
You lit candles for my birthday last week,
and as I stood above their huddle,
I watched the light catch your lips
moistened red by the wine you sipped.

I saw how simple heat is,
how we learn it from our mothers
warming us inside them,
and I thought of those two pans
heat locked, bound together
for the first time.
I want us to be made one,
warmed gently
as I kiss your soles at night
and between your toes
as you lie on your side.

I think of you now at work,
your hands writing on white boards,
your voice projected to the back of the room.
I wonder if you long to stand
under a warm shower
your fingers shaping the water for an instant
and whether you think of me at home,
wanting to press my mouth to the soles of your feet
scented so sweetly I could fall asleep next to them,
heat locked.

## *In And Out Of Light*

Last night I woke every hour
counting them out in my head
my thoughts a dumb numb clock.
I woke you too
and I felt your anger
in my stomach all night.
For half an hour I stood
by the darkened window
thinking of you sleeping
in a blanket of anger across the hall.
My fingers felt along the window sill
hoping to find some way
to let the anger out
of our house for good.
I wanted to throw open the windows
in the dead of winter
and let a Siberian cold
freeze it to the walls and floors.

What wanders these rooms
has never been before.
It is ours to mend or ruin,
and I wanted to stand outside your office door
and listen for your breath
as if it might cross the room bearing
intimate details from your dreams,
but I didn't want to wake you again
so I stayed at the window
searching the night sky
for some hint of the moon.

Finding none, I crawled back to bed
hollowed out my side
and felt over now and then
to your empty side,
drawing my cold hand
up and down the length
as if you were still lying there.
You were so quiet when you left for work
that I woke later
thinking you must have slept in.
I rushed to your office
found it empty, the bed freshly made.
All morning I wandered the house
looking for traces of you
fearing that you had vanished
from my life for good.

In the tree outside the window
a lone magpie flitted from limb to limb
acting as if winter were an ache
it could leave behind
one branch at a time.
Its restlessness troubled me.
I felt its fear through the window
as it hunted for food and danger
the mute air around it tingling with cold.
Finally it flew away to some other tree
down the street
its tiny heart pounding out the day
much like mine does
carrying me one drum beat closer
to the time you return.

I found one of your photos
and a single earring
hanging from your left ear
caught my interest.
You chose the earring yourself and
where to put it
and when to put it there.
I liked that, and I longed
for you to come home
so I could kiss that earring
and your ear lobe
knowing that this love
can never wear out
because we chose each other.
In and out of light we touch
like that earring you made room for.
It touches you and is joined to you
yet it is always an earring too.

On the table are flowers, candles,
one of your favourite meals,
and this poem, white sheets
flat on the green table
yet each word rounded full of love
each vowel a warm shape to the mouth.

## *Living*

For the first time in fifteen years
I take time to watch
light cling
to branches outside.
The branches could be my fingers
spreading pale light
apart in thin strips.
Instead the light
hangs motionless outside
as the sun slides soundless along the horizon.

I wait for you to get off work
to come through the front door
the day already dark
and stand fiddling with keys
just as you did last night
when I filled the house
with candles and flowers.
You thought I'd gone out
until I slipped from the dark
to take your coat
and watch your eyes
flicker in the candle light.
Those flames, unlike the sun,
do not move but are held in place
by thin wicks of waxed string.
We are made of what fuels the flame
and like them
we wait to be extinguished
or to burn down, and out.

I know a young man who has two burial plots,
one from his father's family and one
from his mother's
and he fears he will have to die twice
or have his body halved to please both families.
I wonder about families like that,
already so prepared for death
that living gets in the way.
Our place in the ground is not so important
as what we do when alive
our days marked by the travelling sun
our souls dipped in water not light
yet light attaches to us
makes us visible like those branches
waiting for someone to notice.

I listen to our empty house
and wonder what part of you it holds open.
When you arrive our hands will move
making new shadows as they do
both of us glad
for an evening spent in candle glow
so warm and yellow
we hope it never wears away.

## *A Place To Keep My Words*

When I returned from Vancouver
you gave me a notebook
encased in a cover
you hand crafted.
With two different colours of nail enamel,
you drew a woman's back and hips
and then traced *I Love You*
with your finger.
Another place to keep your words, you said
and I lay it on my desk
where I look at the cover
and see how beauty spreads
from what we hold inside.
I see that your hand was steady
as you traced the words without doubt,
and I've never felt so loved before.
You praise me to others
and I want to praise you too
to show the world how tenderly
you smooth your hands over me
touching me so spontaneously
I hold my breath.

I think of you mixing
nail polish together
silver and gold
to form a new colour, just for me.
You drew lines down the cover;
some lines intersected
other lines didn't

and I trace those lines
fingers meeting where they cross
like ours in the night
fresh from the brow of a dream.

When the book is full
I will slide it next to others
on my bookshelf
and will take it out now and then
to re-read,
finding each time
a different past
to return to.

## Two Digits

My son turned nine yesterday, and on his birthday card I wrote how this was the last year his age would be only one digit. Today, as I drove him to the planetarium for space camp, he said that next year he'd be turning two digits, and then he looked at me and said, *I will never turn three digits,* with a certainty that made me quiver. I answered that I wouldn't either, and then both of us turned silent, as if taking in the weight of such a thought for the first time, the end of our lives suddenly out in the open, too visible, a thought we could never take back, our lives counted out with two digits right to the end.

I wished, then, that I'd written something else on my son's card and hadn't drawn attention to the two digits. Numbers lie just as easily as words, and yet they seem less suspicious, more trustworthy. Only added or subtracted not dressed up with other numbers or embellished like words, one feeding another until the irony seems true, visible. Numbers transform in seconds from one to another through some complex process most of us want to close our eyes on, while words change their meanings slowly, over centuries. What my son said today will mean the same a hundred years from now.

I couldn't stop thinking about my son's words all day, the sad smile on his face, his frankness that frightened me. Perhaps I've prepared him too cruelly for this world, shown him too soon that everyone is mortal. I squeezed his knee the way I wished my father had. Numbers are lies no matter how smoothly they work together, one giving way to another. They are simple lies, powerful lies that let the days be counted, cleanly measured and placed one beside the other, accumulating as if toward some meaning off in the distance we never quite grasp. Next year my son's age will be two digits and his death won't seem so far away anymore, visible right there in the numbers.

## *A Heaven Filled With Snow*

I wandered out in a blizzard
when I was five.
I opened the door in my sleep
and crossed the highway alone.
My father found me
sleeping in a snow bank, but
I remember nothing from that night:
not the cold, nor my father waking me
nor even crossing the highway on my own,
yet I can see it all in my head
footstep by footstep
my hands reaching out to catch snowflakes
as I crossed the busy road
without being struck,
how I stopped and curled under a streetlight
until my father's hot hands slipped under me,
lifted me into his arms
as if I'd just fallen asleep on the couch.

I want to cross a road now
and find my father in snow.
I want to lift him up, just as he did me,
and carry him back into my house
to tell him once more that I love him.

## *Hydrangeas*

You told me
that spring begins
in a word no one can utter.
I hold that word in my head
until I can smell Hydrangeas.
Flowers you brought from the east,
like a taste
my mouth won't ever get used to.
When I finally saw them
I knew there were only a few things
I would ever be gripped by
and their colours
wrung the air with spring.
As it snows today,
the cold can't penetrate
the warmth I found
after a long night breathing spring.
Hydrangeas; how their name
is a moan I can never finish.

*Higher Ground*

## *Beloved*
### *for Pearl*

It drizzles all day in Sooke.
By the window of our new house,
I watch the sea
take back the rain.
Your hand on my neck
rubs through pain.
Last night I turned to you in sleep
and you warmed all the places night chilled.
Rain drummed the roof
and our empty house murmured.

Today waves crest rocks
and my thoughts
follow your fingers as they travel.
Winter stays frozen to the peaks of mountains
across the Strait of Juan de Fuca and the sea
repeats the sky's delicate, worn tones.
I worry that I can describe the ocean
but not your face.
Beloved, your eyes wear
the blues and greens of spring.
You heat muffins in the oven
and walk between empty rooms
planning a future
my heart races toward.

Yesterday a seal poked its face
out of pale water.
We walked to the edge of the rocks
seeking its animal attention.

Patient as the sea, it bobbed
for an usually long time
and watched us with moist, steady eyes.
Today I scan the ocean for that seal
but the water reigns alone.

My thoughts shift from sea
to the tip of your tongue pausing between whispers.
My ears shut out all but the sounds
of us coming home.
I trace a line along the uneven surface
of the strait out into the channel
where a lone freighter
snails toward the open sea.
From our house it looks small
and insignificant just as we must
to anyone on board looking back.
I let this love slip tighter into me.
I turn away from the sea
and kiss you once
as the empty house
settles more firmly into place.

## *Higher Ground*
### *for Pearl, Amanda and Woody*

1

Woody wakes from a nap and calls Amanda
and she answers,
quiet footsteps along the hallway.
I think of Amanda as a girl with you in Mexico.
The two of you sitting on a rooftop
overlooking San Miguel
watching a thin wisp of smoke drift up from
the heart of the city.
Neither of you speaks
merely watch the smoke swell in the heat,
content to do nothing but sit
until the sun goes down.

Woody and Amanda move downstairs.
I catch the odd trill from Woody's play.
What they have might seem common,
but is so rare and beautiful
it never happens twice.
Woody slams a door
and I think of how Breanne and Austin
grew into themselves the same way.
Each child a wave of sounds
rising toward higher ground.

2

Tonight the reading light stretches
our shadows across the bedroom wall.
I hear Woody wake from a nightmare.
Amanda speaks quietly to him
the way I once did with Austin and Breanne
or you with her
quiet loving words
that come on their own
with no prompting.
Our best chance to do some good.

## *The Scientific Measurement Of Love*

*...love, like other psychological constructs, can be studied scientifically, and that, like other psychological constructs, it can also be quantified and measured.*
                                                    *Robert Sternberg*

You can measure love
by standing at a window
and watching rain
renew grass
as farther west, clouds
nearly touch the tops
of spring hungry trees.
A dark rain mutes the city
to tall, shimmering shafts
of granite and glass.

As a boy I walked in the rain and
let it cool the insides of my wrists
while back in the house
my father drank another beer.
Its yellow hue matched the nicotine stains
at the ends of his fingers.
Later at the front door
my dampened hands
slipped on the knob.
My father sat alone,
and his drunken mind
already saw the rain's end.

On the seventh day God rested
and he so loved the world that
he gave his only begotten son
so that we might find everlasting love
and how do you measure that,
squeeze love between fingers
until the raw insides explode?
We think of that God
when we stand in a child's room
and watch their chests heavy with sleep.

Love grows outside the body
and addresses the air
with music or scent.
Love brightens a room
flattened by stale noon light.
Love is spoken
with the bare flicker of words.

That day I walked down the road
toward the highway,
I snapped my fingers in the rain.
I was a teenager looking
for the place inside me
where love could take hold.
I didn't feel the dampness at all
as I walked on the hump of tall grass
that ribbed the center of the road
between worn tire tracks.
As my feet trampled stalks,
I let the rain surround me.

When I got to the highway
I turned around and walked back,
my hands tucked into pockets.
I knew by the time I reached the house,
my father would have
started another beer.

I hoped that if I walked
down to the highway and back
in the rain enough times
my father would be
waiting for me
sober as morning.

## *All In The Family*
### *for Noni and David*

David eloquently explains
how he has fathers
all over the country.
His hands accompany his words
and when he pauses
they settle around his wine glass.
He tells us a dream of his dead father.
Every detail vivid
as his father and brother toss a football,
something they never did while alive.
His hands join in and
I suspect he wonders too
what they are saying.

Matters of the heart are not captured
through words, formulas or theories
but in the simple arcs
hands draw in the air
between sips of wine.
I watch my own hands
try to imagine what they say
but give in to the pull of wine
watch David's instead.
They flick in and out of shadow
and come to rest on the table.
Although not much older,
David could be a father for me too
his well lived hands guiding me
to the far side of grief.

## Singing In Traffic
### *for Austin*

When I drop my son off at daycare,
I have the urge to spend the day with him,
to follow him around so I can see
how he acts when I'm not there.
Sometimes when he plays he seems
a creature all of his own making
and his father makes no sense at all.
Other times, when he sits on my lap
watching TV, I wonder will I become him
one day, young and hopeful again.
All I see now are lives thrown
apart by wind, earth or war
and children lie alone at night
as around them the world is
altered by too many dreams or not enough.
We fail every day, our children
coming home in the rain are still hopeful
even though each day at school
requires them to give in.

When I pick him up after work,
he is angry and I try to calm him.
He throws himself on the floor
crying and I stand over him
afraid to watch what his anger does.
My own anger slips out too easily.
He continues to cry, shaped
more by that than by me.

We walk holding hands to the car
and he looks into the sky,
laughs as a flock of birds
swoops down from the afternoon sky.
He sings a song as the car
moves out into traffic
and I join him forgetting how little I know
about the mysteries of his day.
From the back seat his voice drowns out mine
and slowly I stop singing altogether
and just listen for sounds in his voice
I once tried to place there
with a kiss but couldn't.
He sings as
the traffic around us
forms the frayed edges
of a different world.
At a red light Austin stops singing
and looks at the faces
in the car next to ours
and laughs saying
"Look dad there's people in that car
just like us and they're singing too."

I don't look in their direction
making sure to be polite,
so I never learn if he is right.
I drive on anyway
waiting eagerly for him to start
singing again knowing
I can never ask him to
without thinking of those people
and knowing it's not the proof
I lack but the courage
to stop what I am doing.

He doesn't sing the rest
of the way home
and I look for his face
now and then
in the rear view mirror.
I watch him sit there
his eyes sometimes open
other times closed
and in the front seat
I feel alone not able
to close my eyes even once
all the way home.

## *First Day Of School*
### *for Breanne*

She looks afraid
not of me but of the camera
as I snap a picture.
Her eyes squint at what the light brings.
Her fingers point to heaven
as she leaves my side
for what the school yard asks of her.

I watch two boys wrestle
and then I turn to see her
shyly standing with a group of girls
exchanging the old ways.
From the outside, the school
appears harmless but inside
the children scurry to places
where they will stay afraid.

She doesn't want me waiting
at the edge of the school yard like this
although she never looks over to see
if I'm still here.

The children line up
and she does it so naturally I'm frightened.
The two boys continue to tangle
near the fence and a teacher
must separate them.
One of the boys has red hair
like I did as a boy.

Only when Breanne is at the top of the stairs
does she turn back to wave.
Not a long wave but a brief cautious one
just before she vanishes inside the door.

The wipers snap on when I turn the key
and I hear singing
a child's voice reaching notes
she shouldn't be able to.
I search the empty school yard
for shadows. I feel it in my fingers first
and then my mouth but I know
there isn't anything there.

In the picture I took
the school is out of focus
and looks huge behind her.
I count the windows
at her back and imagine
each one a different part of her life.
I see too the question
she asks the camera.
High above her the sky looks pale.
Her hands are closed fists
and I can almost make out
what she is holding.
My tongue caught
in my mouth by surprise.

## Grace Period

The young woman on TV has a crater
the shape of a bar of soap in her left arm.
She droops the arm over the stove cooking
some sausages, her open wound glistens.
She is a junkie living in Vancouver.
As I watch her I see that for some of us
breathing can't fall away to meaning,
that some lives drain to a false shadow.

Her apartment walls are sticky and damp.
As she walks around it,
the camera greedily takes stock
washing it all to a grainy green and grey.
I can't tell what colour her hair is nor her eyes
nor can I take my gaze away from the wound on her arm,
troubled by how little her body means to her.
There is no grace period for her, harmed by a parting.
Death grasps her arm,
rots a gouge clear to the buried bone.
Still she shakes the pan with her good arm
as the other dangles over the stove,
the flesh sliding from bone.
Like her, we wake in lives wounded or born out of love
and undo it all one nightmare at a time.
She is barely twenty, a body ruined by junk.
I want to scream until I break through
all this fishing in bodies
for a love lost in the thickness of flesh.
She can't stop picking at the wound
formed by all that festers inside her.

She talks just like my own daughter
still tentative with adults
answering each question as if she might be sent to bed.
Her life is glimpsed for a second or two then gone
ruled by the flutter of light inside glass.
I never get to her life,
not a sliver of it here, nothing more
than that hole in her arm and how the camera
stays on it a little too long, in disbelief,
fixes on the wound before moving to her face.
She talks to someone behind the camera
about the wound, explains it
like a child does something they've done wrong.
I pull away to my own feet resting on the footstool
and the safety of my life.
I know she's out there, not just lost
in the rewound film,
but cooking sausages
like I do some mornings.

## *Winter*

Winter lines the shelves
of our house and my bare feet cross
carpet and hardwood.
My thoughts are
heavy with waiting
and my feelings
ripple on fingertips.
My tongue
is caught by a sound
it could never make
without you.
I feel your breathing
with my hands.
I wake next to you
wrapped in covers.
Your fingers
ride the air
in a complete
likeness of love.
Your eyes dip
into the light
and I  breathe
your kisses.

## Time Beyond History
### New Poems

## *Time Beyond History*

I got few glimpses into the workings of my father's mind. He talked seldom, more when he was drunk, but then he talked inebriated circles. Every Saturday night my father drank a twenty-four pack of O'keefe Old Vienna. When he was halfway through the case, he would poke his head in my bedroom door and say one of his strange chants like, "Fucker John, your stake is gone, your pack is in the hall, eh" or "All the hills are covered with snow," or "Life in the Finland woods." Strangest of all was, "Robert, what's time beyond history?"

Some of those phrases must have been ones he heard others sing when he was a boy and they sat around an open fire drinking beer or whiskey. Or ones he learned the summers he road the rails west after the depression to work on the farms near Swift Current. Pictures of him as a young man often show him holding a beer up to the camera. I wonder if during those drunken nights he asked his buddies about time beyond history.

I never knew how to answer that question. Most of the time I pretended to be asleep until he gave up and went for another beer. I have always wondered what answer he expected and where the phrase came from. Did he make it up himself or did someone ask him the same question when he was a boy? For years I have been certain that the phrase held some secret to my father's inner life and I wished I'd asked him about it when he was sober.

When we buried him, I was speechless. I realize now I should have said, *time beyond history.* Instead my brother, sister and I quietly dropped the blue vinyl box containing his ashes into the small rectangle opening in the clay the gravediggers had prepared. Whenever I've considered his question I've focused on *history* and *time* and ignored *beyond* altogether. It wasn't until he was dead that I guessed what he really was asking, and by then, he didn't need my answer.

## *Generous Waters*
### *for Don Coles*

He invites me into his house
As he does into his poems with
A friendly outstretched hand
And an infectious laugh that draws me out.
He is where I wish I came from
And where I want to be headed.
His poems explore the reach of love
And we, like him, come
To belong there.

## *Austin Contemplates Death*

Austin once asked me how long the dead are dead. When I answered forever, he asked, how long is that? When I said we never come back he said, how long is that? He then asked how long our cat would be dead for if she died, and would she die soon? When I answered yes, he said, poor kitty, and went back downstairs to play.

## My Father's Bed

For years my father slept in the living room next to the TV while my mother slept in the bedroom. My father would lie in bed until the TV went off the air and then he'd shutoff all the lights and crawl beneath the covers. The bed sagged in the middle and the mattress was older than anything in the house and smelled even older. He made his bed each morning before work, and every two or three weeks stripped the bed so that my mother could wash the sheets. When she carried them to the washer, she held the sheets out in front of her as if they contained too much of him for her to touch. Only when they were clean could she hug them to her, the washed ones left neatly folded at the foot of his bed.

The most vivid image I have of my father is of him sitting with his legs crossed on the edge of that bed smoking a cigarette and drinking a beer as a cloud drifts toward the smoke-yellowed ceiling. He is wearing a hat, and my mother is sitting on the couch next to him. We are all intently watching a TV show with the sound turned down.

## *For The Record*

When a heart goes quiet
another name is
written down somewhere
not to be remembered
but forgotten with the rest
saved carefully on
shelves or in computers
but never consulted
part of what time
leaves behind
evidence that it
can't take everything with it.

Our lives are
measured out in breaths
but lived in hours, days, months.
The only record of us
are the words and deeds
we leave behind.

The sun comes out after
a week of rain
and I watch a boy
make for the park.
If someday he writes notes
on scraps of paper
how many of them
will survive?
Each life is a
memory and nothing more.

## *Chopin's Music*

Chopin leaves his piano
and opens the window
to let in sounds from the street.
A horse and carriage clatter past,
followed by the hurried taps of a woman's heels.
He reaches out to catch
the first drops of an overdue rain.

Behind him the door opens
and she enters.
He doesn't turn to face her
but watches the tops of heads below.
She begins to play and he follows
her fingers' awkward moves
as he runs his own along the windowsill
feeling each damp groove.
He leaves the window open
and joins her.
The noises of their love making
mix with street sounds.
Afterward he returns to the window
to allow her to escape the bed
the music already changing in his head.
George Sand slips out the door
Her heals striking much lighter than before.

## *A Peculiar Stretching of Time*

You are in Taipei while
A winter storm buries
Parked cars under hoary mounds.
I wake when you are going to bed and
When we talk on the phone
Our voices run ahead
Of the transatlantic lag
And we must pause to let
Our words catch up
.
Later like a lover who holds a flower
To the window of her beloved's parting train
You send pictures of trees heavy with leaves
Along motorcycle-busy streets
That have never seen snow drifts, and of
A picnic table fashioned
From a large palm-shaped granite slab and
Encircled by eight smaller stones.

I find signs of you throughout the house.
Your comb next to the sink,
A pile of books on your side of the bed.
A pair of worn gloves
Shaped to the curl of each finger
Waits on the Mexican chest at the front door.
I miss all the times during the day
That you enter my office
And rub the back of my neck.

When you return
The streets will be cleared
The cars dug out.
For now I stay at home
And look at the pictures you send.
You bring the colour to my life.

## All the white rooms

*They turn the color of heaven - James Dickey*

*for my father and mother*

He bent to pick a rose
to give to my mother.
He wore leather
and looked afraid.
As he handed her the rose,
he had no sense of me
or even if he was capable of me
nor did my mother,
still skeptical
about what men wanted.
Later when he became my father,
all his clothes were work clothes,
and my mother still looked for
the man who handed her the rose.
It was him she took a shine to.
Only later, after he died
did he become
someone to love forever.

## *Molasses*

### *for Pearl*

Every morning you wake before me
and open the curtains
so we can watch Ruby Throated hummingbirds
sip at the feeder outside our window.
From bed we can see the arbutus
across the road which stays green all year
and is now filled with finches and towhees.
This spring on Salt Spring Island
is the first since my childhood
where I've noticed spring's daily progress.
Yellow flowers bloom first
followed by blue, then pink,
white, and finally red and purple.
Near our fence the rosemary bush
is distended with blue flowers.
The honeysuckle you transplanted
in October inches up the fence
and nearby lilacs and rhododendrons
are close to bloom.

When I think of you
I think of the lemon rhododendrons
that we saw this spring
blooming in the nursery.
It's flowers not the yellow
of a lemon peel,
but light and creamy
with a hint of lime.
Lavender rises in corner beds
and Stellar jays make
quick visits to our backyard.

Without you I wouldn't know the names
of birds or plants. I wouldn't know
how to trim an eucalyptus plant
or that in other countries they grow to three hundred feet.
I wouldn't know that the bamboo
along the front yard
will some day make a ten foot screen.
I wouldn't know how to collect
three hundred banana and
molasses coloured slugs
by hand from our yard.

Elsewhere in the world
this has been a difficult spring
coming after a brutal winter.
A spring of SARS and the war in Iraq.
War and disease
often arrive in spring,
but from our living room window
it's possible
to see the good
the earth produces.
Without you I would have missed spring.
I would have seen the returning leaves
and nothing else
the rest blurred
by the stretching day
and the warmer spring winds.